ENGLISH
Verbs

A Communicative Course
Using Story Squares

THOMAS SHEEHAN

Library of Congress Cataloging-in-Publication Data
Sheehan, Thomas, 1950–
    English verbs : a communicative course using story squares / Thomas Sheehan
        p. cm.
    ISBN 0-13-035528-3
    1. English language–Verb–Problems, exercises, etc. 2. English
language–Textbooks for foreign speakers. I. Title.
PE1271.S54 1995
428.2'4–dc20   94–33372
                                         CIP

Acquisitions Editor: Nancy L. Leonhardt
Manager of Development Services: Louisa B. Hellegers
Development Editors: Tünde Dewey, Margaret Grant
Assistant Editor: Sheryl Olinsky
Director of Production and Manufacturing: Aliza Greenblatt
Editorial Production / Design Manager: Dominick Mosco
Electronic / Production and Interior design: Paula Williams and Carey Davies
Production Coordinator: Ray Keating

Cover Art: Susan Spellman
Cover Design: Tom Nery
Art Director: Merle Krumper
Interior Art: Susan Spellman, Richard Toglia, and Arnie Ten
Electronic Art / Realia: Todd Ware, Marita Froimson, Don Kilcoyne, Carey Davies

PRENTICE HALL REGENTS
A VIACOM COMPANY

© 1996 by Prentice Hall Regents
Prentice Hall, Inc.
A Division of Simon & Schuster
Upper Saddle River, NJ 07458

Printed in the United States of America

10 9 8 7 6 5 4 3 2 1

ISBN 0-13-035528-3

Prentice Hall International (UK) Limited, London
Prentice Hall of Australia Pty. Limited, Sydney
Prentice Hall Canada, Inc., Toronto
Prentice Hall Hispanoamericana, S.A., Mexico
Prentice Hall of India Private Limited, New Delhi
Prentice Hall of Japan, Inc., Tokyo
Simon & Schuster Asia Pte. Ltd., Singapore
Editora Prentice Hall do Brasil, Ltda., Rio de Janeiro

Printed on Recycled Paper

For Peggy

Acknowledgments

I am grateful to many people for their inspiration and help in the development of this book. First, I would like to thank hundreds of students for using these materials in experimental form. Their feedback has been invaluable. For their reactions to the pilot versions, I would like to thank the following colleagues at the American Language Institute of the University of Toledo: Robert Cox, Joan Holladay, Patrick Kennedy, and Laura Sund. Helpful advice has also come from Susan English and Adelia Danus. Other kinds of support have been received from Carol Butler, Jerry Davis, Deborah Pierce, and Barbara Sayers.

This course builds on ideas developed by many teachers and writers. I am especially grateful to Alexander Lipson for his fluency squares, Phillip L. Knowles and Ruth A. Sasaki for their work with story squares, Mary Clark for her course on the teaching of grammar at the School for International Training, Robert Kinnunen and Edward Licitra for some ideas on the teaching of grammar, N. R. Cattell for some of the tense names used in this course, my parents for their suggestions, and Penny Ur for her helpful book *Grammar Practice Activities: A Practical Guide for Teachers*.

At Prentice Hall Regents, editor Nancy Leonhardt believed in the project. Assistants Terry TenBarge and Sheryl Olinsky gave administrative support. Reviewers Amanda Gillis–Furutaka, Kevin McClure, and Roger E. Winn-Bell Olsen gave helpful guidance. Development editors Tünde Dewey and Samuela Eckstut tightened up the manuscript. Artists Susan Spellman, Arnie Ten and Richard Toglia worked wonders guided only by my crude sketches; Paula Williams and Carey Davies developed the book's final design. Finally, development editor Margaret Grant coordinated myriad details as the book went into and through production.

For keeping me sane during the writing process, I cannot adequately thank my wife, Peggy.

Photograghs

Page 26, courtesy of the Ford Motor Company; pages 84 and 85, courtesy of the Montana Historical Society.

Thomas Sheehan
Toledo, Ohio

⬦ Contents

All the characters in the story squares are fictitious, and any resemblance to actual persons, living or dead, is purely coincidental.

English Verbs: A Communicative Course Using Story Squares is a semester-long, high intermediate ESL grammar course—with a twist. The twist is the stories. The basis for the course, they provide a context for the presentation and practice of grammatical structures. In addition, they serve as a springboard to many interesting topics.

The Story Square

A story square[1] is a one-page illustration of major points of a story. This book has two story squares. The first, presented in Chapter 1, is a sleazy soap opera called "Ronny's Mistake." Chapters 2 through 5 are thematically related to this story. The first hour or so of class time is spent learning the story. (Plot summaries and instructions for the presentation of a story square are in the Teacher's Guide.) Once learned, the story is shared knowledge, a clear context with limited vocabulary, through which grammar points can be presented and practiced. Almost all the examples and many of the exercise items are related to the story in some way. In Chapter 6, students learn the second story, "The Big River Mix-Up," a tale of political scandal. The rest of the book is thematically related to it.

The stories and related topics lighten the tone of the grammar class. Topics suggested by "Ronny's Mistake" include fortune-telling, near-death experiences, and sports cars. Topics related to "The Big River Mix-Up" include Montana history, politics, feral children, and the environmental movement.

The Organization of a Chapter

With the exception of Chapters 1 and 6, which present the story squares, and Chapter 9, each chapter is divided into lessons designed for one, two, or three days of work. Lessons generally consist of the following elements:

The presentation of a grammatical point: This is done through exercises in which students analyze the target structure, through readings, or through examples. Presentation activities are often labeled **Read It!** or **Analyze It!** Grammar is always presented through a context: the story itself or a reading on a topic suggested by the story.

Practice activities: These consist of fill-in-the-blank, transformation, and other kinds of exercises which help students manipulate the target structure. The content of many of the practice items is related to the story squares. These activities are labeled **Practice It!**

Open-ended, communicative activities: Students use the target grammatical structures creatively. They may interview each other, conduct a survey, or solve a problem. These activities are labeled **Use It!** and provide a bridge from the stories to the real world.

---

[1] Lipson boxes, the forerunner of story squares, were first developed by Alexander Lipson for use in Russian classes. In their book *Story Squares* (Winthrop, 1980), Phillip L. Knowles and Ruth A. Sasaki include Lipson boxes, which they call fluency squares, and story squares, but the use of the story squares in that book is quite different from their use here.

Innovative Presentation of Grammar Points

The innovative presentation of grammar points provides a fresh look at English verbs. Some examples are:

1. In Chapter 2, "Power Words," students learn to use auxiliary verbs in questions, negative sentences, short answers, and sentences with *and, so, neither,* and *but*.

2. Chapter 3, "Verb Phrases," is a study of verb forms and their uses. Students learn that certain combinations of verb forms, like "must have gone" are possible in English, while others, like "must had went," are not. Many students have found the simple rules presented in this chapter to be the most useful part of the entire book.

3. The task of mastering sixteen verb tenses is made manageable by the concept of time focuses. There are only three focuses: past, present, and future. Each focus has fewer than seven kinds of tenses (simple, perfect progressive, etc.). A student who understands the relationship between the present-focus tenses (simple present, present perfect progressive, etc.) can see that same relationship in the past focus and the future focus tenses. In essence, the tenses are divided and conquered.

4. Meaningful names for tenses are used instead of confusing traditional names. For example, the present perfect tense is called the before-present tense. In addition, the five forms of verbs (*eat, ate, eaten, eats, eating*) are referred to by number (Form 1, Form 2, etc.). High intermediate students already know numbers in English, and there is no need to burden them with misleading terms like *past participle*. (Indeed, the "past" participle is often used to refer to future or present events: "I will have eaten by the time you get here.")

The Teacher's Guide explains these points completely and gives suggestions for their presentation and practice.

The study of English verb structures is hard for many ESL students. *English Verbs: A Communicative Course Using Story Squares*, however, makes the job easier and more enjoyable. The stories and related topics appeal to students and teachers alike. They provide an attractive means for ESL students to accomplish what they may otherwise see as an onerous task.

The Teacher's Guide

Teachers using this book must have the summaries of the story-square plots, which can be found in the Teacher's Guide. In addition, the Teacher's Guide includes:

1. Techniques for the presentation of the story squares.
2. Suggestions for the presentation and practice of grammar points.
3. Guidelines for many of the activities throughout the book.
4. More in-depth discussion of many grammar points than are found in the students' book. This information is intended to help you answer students' questions.
5. Answer keys.
6. Correction symbols that encourage students to correct their own errors.

To the Student

This is a grammar book. It's also a kind of story book with two stories.
The first story, a soap opera, is in Chapter 1. The second story, a
political scandal, is in Chapter 6.

It's important for you to know the stories well because most of the
grammatical examples and many of the activities are related to them.
The stories provide a clear context to help you understand the meaning
of the grammatical structures.

RONNY'S MISTAKE
LEARNING THE STORY

Activity 1   *Get the Background!*

Look at the story square on page 2 and read this introduction.

The first story, "Ronny's Mistake," is about a man named Ronny who makes a terrible mistake. It's a mystery story.

Ronny, Lonnie, Burl, and Pearl are the main characters[1] in the story. Two minor characters[2] are a lawyer named Mr. Finster and a fortune teller[3] named Madame Vista. You and your classmates are part of the story too. You are detectives.[4]

The story began in April of last year, and it's still going on today. In April, all these people were living in Appleton, a small town in Indiana, USA. Pearl was working in a bank. Ronny was a real estate agent.[5] It's not clear what kind of work Lonnie and Burl were doing, if any.

Some of the characters know each other very well. In fact, some are even in the same family. Some don't know each other at all. As detectives, you need to discover the relationships between them.

In April, something happened that changed the lives of these people. You need to find out what happened and how it changed their lives.

Vocabulary

[1] main character: an important person in a story
[2] minor character: a less important person in a story
[3] fortune teller: a person who can tell people about their futures
[4] detective: someone, often a police officer, who tries to solve mysteries
[5] real estate agent: a business person who buys and sells buildings and land

RONNY'S MISTAKE

Activity 2   *Get More Facts!*

Read these major points about the story as you study the pictures.

In April of last year:

Picture 1:   When Ronny asked Madame Vista, a fortune teller, for advice, she told him there would be a dangerous woman in his future.

Picture 2:   Lonnie fell in love with one of the shooters at a shooting match.

Picture 3:   Burl surprised himself by winning a prize in a shooting match.

Picture 4:   In a meeting with a lawyer, Mr. Finster, Pearl learned that she had inherited[1] seven million dollars and that she had to share that money with her brother.

In May of last year:

Picture 5:   Ronny paid somebody seventy-five thousand dollars in advance.[2]

Picture 6:   On May 7, Lonnie made an important phone call.

Picture 7:   On May 6, Burl left for a cruise[3] around the world.

Picture 8:   Pearl was seriously injured in an attack.

Now:

Picture 9:   Unhappy and confused, Ronny is thinking about ways to improve his life.

Picture 10: Lonnie is enjoying her new sports car.

Picture 11: Burl is thinking about marrying someone who has a lot of money.

Picture 12: Pearl is playing tennis.

Next year:

Pictures 13 to 16:   The future is never sure!

Activity 3   *Discuss It!*

You have read the major points about the story, but there is still a lot you don't know. In small groups, discuss these questions.

1. Do you have any ideas about the relationships between the characters?
2. What do you think you need to know to understand the story completely?

Vocabulary

[1] to inherit: to receive money from someone who has died
[2] in advance: before somebody does a job
[3] a cruise: a trip on a beautiful ship

Activity 4   *Learn the Whole Story!*

On a sheet of paper, write one or two *yes/no* questions that you can ask your teacher to learn more about Ronny, Lonnie, Burl, Pearl, Mr. Finster, and Madame Vista. Ask your teacher your questions. Ask as many questions as you think you need to understand the story completely.

> **Examples:**
>
> **Student 1:**   *In Picture 6, did Lonnie call Burl?*
> **Teacher:**   *No, she didn't.*
>
> **Student 2:**   *In Picture 12, is Pearl feeling better these days?*
> **Teacher:**   *Yes, she is. She's almost back to normal.*

Activity 5   *Double-Check It!*

Listen as your teacher reads each question. Then write the question and check (✔) the best answer.

> **Example:**
>
> **Teacher:**   *Who did Pearl talk with in April of last year?*
>
> **Students write:**   *Who did Pearl talk with in April of last year?*

a. ☐ Burl.   b. ☐ Lonnie.   c. ☑ A lawyer.

1. _____

_____

a. ☐ Yes, he did.   b. ☐ No, he didn't.   c. ☐ Yes, she did.

2. _____

_____

a. ☐ Burl.   b. ☐ Pearl.   c. ☐ Ronny.

3. _____

_____

a. ☐ Pearl.   b. ☐ Burl.   c. ☐ Lonnie.

4. _____

a. ☐ Pearl.   b. ☐ Burl.   c. ☐ Lonnie.

5. _____

    a. ☐ He thought she might kill him to get all the money.
    b. ☐ He knew that he was a good shot with a pistol.
    c. ☐ He didn't fear her.

6. _____

    a. ☐ Lonnie.   b. ☐ Pearl.   c. ☐ Burl.

7. _____

    _____

    a. ☐ Pearl told her.
    b. ☐ She called Ronny, and he told her.
    c. ☐ Burl told her.

8. _____

    a. ☐ Ronny.   b. ☐ Burl.   c. ☐ Pearl.

9. _____

    _____

    a. ☐ He's in love with her.
    b. ☐ She's rich.
    c. ☐ He can't marry Pearl.

10. _____

    a. ☐ He invited Burl to go on a cruise.
    b. ☐ He thought the fortune teller was talking about Pearl, but she was really talking about Lonnie.
    c. ☐ She fell in love with the wrong man.

Chapter 2

POWER WORDS

 **Lesson 1**

Power Word Basics

Point to Remember: Identifying Power Words[1] ....

Power words are words like *does*, *are*, and *have*. Power words are one of the keys to English verb structures.

Activity 1   *Analyze It!*

Find the power word in each sentence by changing the sentence to a *yes/no* question. The first word of the question is the power word.

Example:

Ronny went to a fortune teller last year.
Did *Ronny go to a fortune teller last year?* (***Did*** *is the power word.*)

1. Ronny is bald.
2. Burl practices every day.
3. Lonnie fell in love with Burl.
4. Pearl is playing tennis.
5. Pearl has a brother.
6. Burl has been shooting for many years.
7. Lonnie has to take good care of her new car.
8. Ronny had to pay the fortune teller.
9. Lonnie's got a car.
10. Ronny should have asked the fortune teller more questions.

Point to Remember: Groups of Power Words ....

There are four groups of power words. When you complete the table in Activity 2, you will have the complete list of power words in American English. There are no others.

---

[1] The traditional name for these words is *auxiliary verbs*.

Activity 2   *Analyze It!*

As a class, list all the power words below. Your teacher will write the lists on the blackboard.

Have power words: a. _____*have*_____   **Modal** power words: a. _____*can*_____
                     b. _____   b. _____
                     c. _____   c. _____

Do power words: a. _____   d. _____
                   b. _____   e. _____
                   c. _____   f. _____

Be power words: a. _____   g. _____
                   b. _____   h. _____
                   c. _____   i. _____
                   d. _____   j. _____
                   e. _____

Points to Remember: The Power Words *Do* and *Have* •••••••••••••••••••

1   Power words in sentences with *have* are sometimes hard to identify.

    a. Pearl has a brother. (Power word: *does*)[1]
    b. Burl has been shooting for many years. (Power word: *has*)
    c. Lonnie has to take good care of her new car. (Power word: *does*)
    d. Ronny had to pay the fortune teller. (Power word: *did*)

2   The power words *have*, *has*, and *had* occur only in verb phrases with a past participle.

                    past participle
    a. Fortune tellers have <u>advised</u> many people.   (Power word: *have*)

         past participle
    b. Lonnie's <u>got</u> a new car.[2] (Power word: *has*)

3   Use the power words *do*, *does*, and *did* in all other cases. This will help you to avoid mistakes.

    a. Lonnie **has** a new car. (Power word: *does*)

    b. Burl **had** to practice a lot before his match. (Power word: *did*)

---

[1] Although it is often possible to use a power word from the *have* family in sentences like this, students can avoid mistakes by using the *do* family of power words when possible.

[2] The meaning of this sentence is the same as "Lonnie has a new car." The power word is different.

Activity 3   *Practice It!*

Work with a partner. Student 1 makes a *yes/no* question from the sentence given. Student 2 gives a true short answer using a power word.

Example:

You love sports cars.

Student 1:   *Do you love sports cars?*
Student 2:   *Yes, I do.*

On July 20, 1969, Neil Armstrong became the first human to walk on the the moon.

1. You have consulted a fortune teller.
2. Ronny has explained his mistake to Pearl.
3. You had to visit the school office yesterday.
4. You have a crystal ball.
5. You have to go to the bank tomorrow.
6. Men had walked on the moon before you were born.
7. The person next to you has a hat on.
8. You had studied power words before you took this class.
9. You had to make an important trip last year.
10. Your brother's got a sports car.

Points to Remember: Visible and Invisible Power Words · · · · · · · · · · · · · · ·

❶ There are two kinds of power words: **visible** and **invisible**. A power word is visible if it can be seen in a sentence.

Examples with visible power words:

a. Pearl **may** someday forgive Ronny.
   (You can see the power word *may* in this sentence.)

b. Ronny **has** been paying Lonnie thousands every month.
   (You can see the power word *has* in this sentence.)

❷ In many affirmative sentences, you cannot see the power word; it is invisible.

Examples with invisible power words:

a. Ronny got his half of his uncle's money.
   (The power word is *did*, but you cannot see it in this sentence.)

b. Pearl plays tennis as often as possible.
   (The power word is *does*, but it is invisible in this sentence.)

Activity 4   *Analyze It!*

Step 1:   Identify the power word in each sentence. Then check (✔) *visible* or *invisible*.

Examples:

Burl ate too much during his cruise.
Power word: _____ *did* _____   ☐ visible   ✔ invisible

Ronny is very confused about his situation.
Power word: _____ *is* _____   ✔ visible   ☐ invisible

1. Ronny should get some good advice from somebody.
    Power word: _____   ☐ visible   ☐ invisible

2. Some people in this class can speak more than two languages.
    Power word: _____   ☐ visible   ☐ invisible

3. Exercise helps people to improve their condition.
    Power word: _____   ☐ visible   ☐ invisible

4. Burl has used up almost all his money.
    Power word: _____   ☐ visible   ☐ invisible

5. A monument was built for soldiers who died in the last war.
    Power word: _____   ☐ visible   ☐ invisible

6. Some fortune tellers use special cards to see into the future.
    Power word: _____   ☐ visible   ☐ invisible

7. It is against the law to take towels from a hotel.
    Power word: _____   ☐ visible   ☐ invisible

8. A good lawyer might be able to help Ronny.
    Power word: _____   ☐ visible   ☐ invisible

9. People from many countries have to get a visa before they travel to the USA.
    Power word: _____   ☐ visible   ☐ invisible

10. Burl's ship traveled from New York to Liverpool in five days.
    Power word: _____   ☐ visible   ☐ invisible

Step 2:   Now fill in the blanks below.

Only three power words can be invisible. They are: _____,
_____, and _____. All other power words are **always** visible.

◈ Lesson 2

Power Words in Negative Sentences and **Yes/No Questions**

Point to Remember: Negative Sentences ●●●●●●●●●●●●●●●●●●●●●●●●●●●●●●●●●●●●●

The power word is always the word before *not* in a negative sentence.

    a. Burl did not kill Pearl.
       (Power word: *did*)

    b. Most people cannot see pictures in a crystal.
       (Power word: *can*)

Activity 5   *Practice It!*

Change each affirmative sentence to a negative sentence about someone in your classroom.

Example:

Lonnie received a check from Ronny.
My teacher did not receive a check from Ronny.

  1. Burl keeps a gun under his pillow.
  2. Madame Vista can see pictures in a crystal ball.
  3. Madame Vista foretells the future.
  4. Pearl spent three months in the hospital last year.
  5. Burl should leave town immediately.
  6. Lonnie drives a red sports car.
  7. Burl gained a lot of weight last year.
  8. Pearl enjoys cooking.
  9. Burl has broken many laws.
10. Ronny and Pearl are brother and sister.

Activity 6   *Use It!*

Work with a partner. Choose one of the characters in "Ronny's Mistake." First, write a sentence explaining whom you are writing about. Then, write seven negative sentences that show differences between your partner and the character that you have chosen. Check your sentences with your partner to be sure they are true. Use each of these power words: *does, did, has, is, was, can,* and *will.*

Example:

My sentences show the differences between Lee and Burl.
Lee doesn't know how to shoot a gun.

Point to Remember: *Yes/No Questions and Short Answers* ··················

As you saw in Activities 1 and 3, the first word in every *yes/no* question is a power word. Also, short answers to *yes/no* questions often contain power words.

    a. **Q: Does** Ronny regret his actions?
       A: Yes, he **does**.

    b. **Q: Can** fortune tellers really see into the future?
       A: Maybe they **can**.

Activity 7   *Use It!*

Work with a partner. In numbers 1 through 5, Student 1 asks a *yes/no* question using the word given. Student 2 answers with a true short answer. In numbers 6 through 10, students reverse roles. Use each of the following power words at least once: *do, does, did, has, is, was, can,* and *will.* Write down your questions and answers as shown in the example.

Example: cruise

Andy: *Have you ever taken a cruise?*
Sonia: *No, I haven't.*

1. breakfast	5. sports	8. cook
2. believe	6. travel	9. alcohol
3. serious	7. joke	10. fortune teller
4. uncle		

Lesson 3

Power Words in Wh- *Questions*

Points to Remember: *Wh- Phrases* ···································

❶   *Wh-* questions are questions that begin with **wh- phrases**. A *wh-* phrase may consist of one or more words.

    a. **Who** took Pearl to the hospital?
    b. **What kind of operation** was performed on Pearl?
    c. **Which man** is responsible for this terrible crime?
    d. **How long** will Pearl need to take medication?[1]

---

[1] Even though the word *how* does not begin with *wh-*, questions beginning with *how* are considered *wh-* questions.

❷ Sometimes the *wh-* phrase is the subject of the question. In the examples below, **S** means subject.

             S
   a. <u>Who</u> took Pearl to the hospital?
                  S
   b. <u>What kind of operation</u> was performed on Pearl?

❸ Other times, the *wh-* phrase is not the subject. Another word is the subject.

                S
   a. Why did <u>doctors</u> have to operate on Pearl?
                   S
   b. Whose house did <u>Pearl</u> stay in during her recuperation?

Activity 8   *Analyze It!*

Underline the complete *wh-* phrase in each question below. Then, write an *S* above the subject of the question.

    Examples:

        S
    <u>Whose ex-boyfriend</u> has just returned from a cruise?

               S
    <u>How many countries</u> did Burl visit on his cruise?

   1. What happened to Pearl?
   2. Which students have driver's licenses?
   3. How many miles has Pearl's attacker traveled?
   4. Where can you get your car repaired?
   5. How much money was spent on medicine in your country last year?
   6. Why is it important to be able to find the subject in a question?

Point to Remember: Two Types of *Wh-* Questions ·····························

There are two types of *wh-* questions. In Type One questions, the *wh-* phrase is the subject. In Type Two questions, the *wh-* phrase is not the subject.

Activity 9   *Analyze It!*

Fill in the blanks.

In Activity 8 above, the *wh-* phrase is the subject in questions numbers _____, _____, and _____. Therefore, those questions are Type One *wh-* questions. On the other hand, the *wh-* phrase is not the subject in questions numbers _____, _____, and _____. Therefore, those questions are Type Two questions.

Points to Remember: Type One *Wh-* Questions ·······························

❶ In Type One *wh-* questions, the *wh-* phrase is the subject. If the power word is *do*, *does*, or *did*, it is usually invisible.

> **Q:** Who collects $10,000 from Ronny every month? (Invisible power word: *does*)
> **A:** Lonnie. *or* Lonnie does.

> **Q:** What happened to Pearl? (Invisible power word: *did*)
> **A:** She was attacked.

❷ All other power words are always visible in Type One *wh-* questions.

> **Q:** Who **is** driving a car? (Visible power word: *is*)
> **A:** Lonnie. *or* Lonnie is.

> **Q:** Whose brother **should** tell her everything? (Visible power word: *should*)
> **A:** Pearl's. *or* Pearl's should.

Activity 10 *Practice It!*

Put the verb in the correct tense. Put one or two words in each blank. Use a power word if necessary.

Example:

> **Q:** Who ___*shot*___ (shoot) Pearl?
> **A:** Burl did.

1. **Q:** Who _____ (try) to forget his past right now?
   A: Ronny is.
2. **Q:** Whose car _____ (be) bright red?
   A: Lonnie's is.
3. **Q:** What _____ (cause) the greatest number of disagreements?
   A: Money does.
4. **Q:** Who _____ (prepare) the food on a cruise ship?
   A: The cook does.
5. **Q:** Who _____ (consult) an advisor?
   A: People with problems should.
6. **Q:** What _____ (keep) people's feet dry in wet weather?[1]
   A: Boots do.
7. **Q:** Which company _____ (produce) the greatest number of computers?
   A: IBM does.

---

[1] The question words *who* and *what* almost always take a singular verb. **Exception:** Questions with the verb *be* like "What are those?" and "Who were they?"

8. **Q:** Which part of the world _____(industrialize) the most quickly in recent years?

   A: The Pacific Rim has.

9. **Q:** What _____(save) the most gasoline?

   A: Driving slower will.

10. **Q:** Who _____(tell) Ronny to look out for a dangerous woman?

    A: The fortune teller did.

Activity 11   *Use It!*

Work with a partner. Student 1 asks a question with *who* and the word or words given. Student 2 answers truthfully with the name of a third student in the class and a power word. Student 2 can answer with "nobody" if necessary. Use many different power words.

   Example: *late*

   Q: *Who came to class late today?*
   A: *Sandra did.   or   Nobody did.*

1. curly	4. from Asia	7. plays	10. red
2. straight	5. from (country)	8. between	11. near
3. tennis shoes	6. February	9. blue eyes	12. questions

Point to Remember: Type Two *Wh-* Questions •

In Type Two *wh-* questions, the *wh-* word is not the subject. Every Type Two *wh-* question has a visible power word.

               s
   Q: What do people do on cruise ships?

   A: They often flirt!

              s
   Q: Why did Ronny hire Burl?

   A: He was scared.

Activity 12   *Practice It!*

When Pearl was attacked, she had a near-death experience, or NDE. Doctors believed that she had died. Then she returned to life. Read each sentence. Then make a Type Two *wh-* question that can be answered by the *italicized* words. Use each of the following *wh-* words at least once. Use a power word from the *do* family when possible.

how	what	when	whose
how long	what color	where	why
how often	what kind of	whom	

Pearl was attacked *in her driveway.*

Where was Pearl attacked?

1. Pearl found herself floating *above her body* after the attack.
2. She saw *her body* in the driveway.
3. Suddenly, she was zooming *toward a bright light.*
4. The light was *white.*
5. She was zooming *for several seconds.*
6. She met *a very gentle man.*
7. She felt *peaceful.*
8. She felt peaceful *because everything was beautiful.*
9. The man asked her *whether she wanted to stay or go back.*
10. She knew *that she had to go back to her life.*
11. She woke up *in the hospital.*
12. The doctors had thought *that she would die.*
13. Her life has been different *since that time.*
14. It is better *because she is happy now.*
15. She feels *calm* most of the time.
16. She *almost never* gets angry.
17. Thousands of people have had *the same kind of* experience.
18. Many have reported *seeing the bright light.*
19. They can understand *Pearl's* experiences.
20. Scientists have to study *this phenomenon.*

Activity 13 *Practice It!*

Make a *wh-* question for each answer given. Use the *do* family of power words when possible.

Example:

A fortune teller. (A fortune teller talked to Ronny about a dangerous woman.)
Who talked to Ronny about a dangerous woman?

1. One. (Pearl has one brother.)
2. One. (One doctor works in that clinic.)
3. In a hotel in Sitka, Alaska. (Burl spent the night of May 10 in a hotel in Sitka, Alaska.)
4. A letter. (The secretary typed a letter for Mr. Finster.)
5. Fear did. (Fear caused Ronny to hire Burl.)
6. Mine. (My test was the best in the class.)
7. Mr. Mohammad's. (Mr. Mohammad's poem won the prize.)
8. Seat belts do. (Seat belts save thousands of lives every year.)
9. By scoring a goal in the last twenty seconds. (Ko Wah won the game by scoring a goal in the last twenty seconds.)
10. Tomorrow. (We have to hand in the composition tomorrow.)
11. Florida. (Pearl and Ronny's mother moved to Florida.)
12. Ronny and Pearl's mother. (Ronny and Pearl's mother moved to Florida.)
13. Because it shrank. (Nyuk Tsin gave that blouse to her little sister because it shrank.)
14. The expensive one. (We bought the expensive sofa.)
15. The expensive one. (The expensive sofa seems more comfortable.)
16. Several. (Ronny has watched several videos today.)

17. Every three or four weeks. (Pearl has a party every three or four weeks.)
18. Drinks and snacks. (Pearl has to buy drinks and snacks for her party.)
19. Ronny and Pearl's did. (Ronny and Pearl's dad died about three years ago.)
20. Three years ago. (Pearl and Ronny's dad died about three years ago.)

Activity 14   *Practice It!*

Step 1:   Read the passage about the history of crystal balls.

Using crystal balls to see pictures of the future is an ancient[1] art, probably as ancient as humanity itself. Even before the invention of glass, religious leaders often looked for images[2] in the clear water of rivers or lakes. When they saw images, they studied them—like pictures on Tarot cards[3]—for their special meanings. For example, a village chief looking into a river might have seen an image of a warrior in full battle dress. This image meant that his enemy was going to attack him.

With the invention of glass, people started looking into crystals. Crystals were used by ancient Greek seers.[4] At Delphi, for example, a priestess[5] named Pythia probably used crystals to predict the future for kings, generals, or anyone else making important plans. In other lands, religious leaders carried crystals with them at all times. They thought that looking into the crystals allowed them to communicate with the dead.

Fortune tellers around the world predict the future in many ways. In some places, a seer throws small bones on a table and reads the pattern[6] that they make. Fortune tellers in other cultures read people's hands, feet, and heads. Still others read tea leaves or cards. Almost anyone can learn these skills, but only a clairvoyant can see pictures in a crystal. The French word clairvoyant means "clear sight," and people who have this kind of clear sight can see pictures that average people cannot. This special talent is quite rare; it is a real gift.

Step 2:   Discuss these questions.
1. What did primitive people really see in the water?
2. Do you believe that some people can see pictures of the future?
3. Why did everybody consult the seers at the famous Greek oracles?
4. Is it possible to communicate with the dead?
5. Do you know anyone who can read palms, cards, or tea leaves?

Vocabulary

[1] ancient: very old
[2] image: a picture
[3] tarot cards: special cards for telling fortunes
[4] seer: someone who can see the future
[5] priestess: a female religious leader
[6] pattern: a design

Step 3: Write questions for the answers given below. Use only these *wh-* words: *who, what, how, where, why.* The answers are in the same order that they appear in the story.

Example:

Probably as ancient as humanity.
How old is the art of the crystal ball?

1. In the clear water of rivers or lakes.
2. That his enemy was going to attack him.
3. At Delphi.
4. She was a famous priestess.
5. Pythia did.

6. Because they thought that the crystals allowed them to communicate with the dead.
7. A seer does.
8. Almost anyone can.
9. "Clear sight."
10. Quite.

Activity 15   *Use It!*

Step 1: Pretend you are someone else. Choose one of the identities below—or think of some other interesting identity.

- the father or mother of four sets of twins
- a lion tamer
- Christopher Columbus
- the world's tallest person
- the lighting expert for a popular rock band

- somebody who has just returned to civilization after twenty years alone on an island
- the manager of an international airport
- an invisible person
- a Supermodel

Step 2: Choose a partner. Interview your partner in her/his new identity. Your partner will interview you, too. Don't be afraid to use your imagination when you answer questions. For example, if you are Christopher Columbus, but you don't know all the facts about his life, you can make up an answer. This is a grammar class, not a history class.

Step 3: Write up the interview in question-and-answer form. Write at least ten questions and answers. Use a variety kinds of questions and power words. (**Note:** You do not have to write down every question that you asked. Include only the interesting ones.)

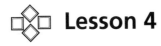 **Lesson 4**

Power Words in Tag Questions

Points to Remember: Tag Questions ••

➊ We use tag questions to check information. The following are examples of things Madame Vista might have said to Ronny.

After affirmative sentences:

a. **Madame Vista:** You have a sister, **don't you?**
   Ronny: Yes, I do.

b. **Madame Vista:** You have seen your sister this week, **haven't you?**
   Ronny: No, I haven't.

After negative sentences:

c. **Madame Vista:** You don't have a sister, **do you?**
   Ronny: Yes, I do.

d. **Madame Vista:** You haven't seen your sister this week, **have you?**
   Ronny: No, I haven't.

❷ Affirmative and negative tag questions are answered in the same way. Ronny has a sister, so he answers "yes" in a. and c. above. Similarly, he hasn't seen Pearl recently, so he answers "no" in b. and d.

Activity 16 *Analyze It!*

Analyze the structure of the examples above and answer these questions.

1. Does every tag question have a visible power word?

   ☐ Yes   ☐ No

2. After an affirmative sentence, is the tag question affirmative or negative?

   ☐ Affirmative   ☐ Negative

3. After a negative sentence, is the tag question affirmative or negative?

   ☐ Affirmative   ☐ Negative

4. Ronny paid Burl, didn't he?

   ☐ Yes, he did.
   ☐ No, he didn't.

5. Ronny didn't pay Burl, did he?

   ☐ Yes, he did.
   ☐ No, he didn't.

Activity 17 *Practice It!*

Step 1: Madame Vista is gazing into her crystal ball and telling you about yourself. She uses a lot of tag questions because, although she believes in herself, she is not really 100 percent sure about what she sees. Add a tag question to five of the sentences below. Use the *do* power words when possible.

Step 2: Answer the question truthfully about yourself. Give a little extra information to explain your answer.

Step 3: Change the sentence to a negative sentence with an affirmative tag question.

Step 4: Answer the new question truthfully but do not repeat the extra information.

Example: You come from a big family.

Madame: You come from a big family, don't you?
You: Yes, I do. I have six brothers and five sisters.

or

Madame: You don't come from a big family, do you?
You: Yes, I do.

1. You live in a tall building.
2. Both your grandfathers are still alive.
3. You've been having trouble sleeping.
4. You get a lot of exercise.
5. You have a slight pain in your shoulder.
6. You were born in the same month as your father.
7. You are sure about your future career.
8. You are in love.
9. You have recently had a death in your family.
10. Your brothers and sisters are all still in school.

Activity 18 *Use It!*

Step 1: Get to know your classmates better. Write down three affirmative hunches and two negative hunches about five different students. Use five different power words. Add a tag question to each hunch. Leave a space to write your classmates' answers.

Example:

Me: Fang, you live with your sister, don't you?
Fang:

Step 2: Tell your classmates your hunches. Use tag questions. Then write down their answers. If an answer is "no," get an explanation as in the example. If an answer is "yes," no explanation is necessary.

Example:

Me: Fang, you live with your sister, don't you?
Fang: No, I don't. I live with my two brothers.

Step 3: Read your mini-dialogues out loud with your classmates.

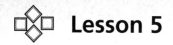

Lesson 5

Power Words with And, So, Neither, and But

Points to Remember: Power Words in Combining Ideas ·····················

❶ To combine two similar affirmative ideas, we can use *and so* and a power word.

a. Burl got money from Ronny last year, **and so did** Lonnie.

= $\left\{ \begin{array}{l} \text{Burl got money from Ronny last year.} \\ + \\ \text{Lonnie got money from Ronny last year.} \end{array} \right.$

b. **Burl:**   You've changed.
   Lonnie: **So have** you.

❷ To combine two similar negative ideas, we can use *and neither* and a power word.

a. Ronny has never had a near death experience (NDE), **and neither has** Lonnie.

= $\left\{ \begin{array}{l} \text{Ronny has never had an NDE.} \\ + \\ \text{Lonnie has never had an NDE.} \end{array} \right.$

b. **Madame Vista:**   I don't know who the dangerous woman is.
   Ronny: **Neither do** I.

❸ To combine negative and affirmative ideas, we use *but* and a power word.

a. Pearl feels calm most of the time, **but** Ronny **doesn't.**
b. Lonnie didn't consult Madame Vista, **but** Ronny **did.**
c. **Burl:**   I have to get more money somewhere.
   Lonnie: **But** I **don't.**

Activity 19 *Practice It!*

Put *and, so, neither, but,* or a power word in each blank. Your answers must be true.

Example:

Accountants need to understand math, __and__ __so__ __do__ engineers.

1. Burl has broken the law, _____ _____ _____ Lonnie.
2. It is hot in Nigeria, _____ it _____ not in Antarctica.
3. Ronny is being blackmailed, _____ Burl _____ not.
4. Babies cannot survive without help from their parents, _____ _____ _____ young animals.
5. Burl doesn't seem very nice, _____ _____ _____ his girl friend.
6. Eggs give you a lot of protein, _____ _____ _____ milk.
7. Pearl's life has changed for the better, _____ Ronny's _____ not.

8. Confucius tried to bring peace to the world, _____ _____ _____ Gandhi.
9. Lonnie has long hair, _____ Pearl _____ not.
10. Mechanics don't usually keep their hands clean, _____ nurses _____.

Activity 20 *Use It!*

Step 1: Write six personal *yes/no* questions that you would like to ask some of your classmates. You may use the words below if you like. Use a different power word in each question. (**Note:** Leave the four columns on the right side of the table blank for now.)

roommate	basketball	jokes	Washington	scorpion
contact lenses	blue jeans	messy	hospital	farm
application	grandfather	fraternity	laundry	whale

Example: roller coaster

Questions	Names	Y/N?	Names	Y/N?
Have you ever ridden a roller coaster?				
1.				
2.				
3.				
4.				
5.				
6.				

Step 2: Walk around and ask classmates your questions. Record their answers on the chart. (**Note:** Continue asking different students until you get two questions with answers *yes/yes*, two with *no/no*, and two with *yes/no*.)

Example:

Questions	Names	Y/N?	Names	Y/N?
Have you ever ridden a roller coaster?	*Jack*	*N*	*Mary*	*Y*

Step 3: Write six true sentences about the students you interviewed. Write two sentences with *so*, two with *neither*, and two with *but*.

Example:

Jack has never ridden a roller coaster, but Mary has.

VERB PHRASES

 Lesson 1

Verb Phrases and the Five Verb Forms

Points to Remember: Five Verb Forms •

❶ Verb phrases usually contain from one to four words.

One word: Ronny **went** to a fortune teller.
Two words: Lonnie **has bought** a new car.
Three words: Pearl's doctor **must have been** excellent.
Four words: Lonnie **might have been watching** TV last night at 9:00.

❷ Some things are possible in English verb phrases, and others are not.

Possible: might have been watching
Impossible: might have being watching

❸ Except for the verb *be* all verbs in English have five forms. These are the forms for irregular verbs.

Form 1	Form 2	Form 3	Form 4	Form 5
drive	drove	driven	drives	driving
have	had	had	has[1]	having
shoot	shot	shot	shoots	shooting

❹ Except for the verbs *be* and *have*, only Forms 2 and 3 can be irregular.

❺ These are the forms for regular verbs.

Form 1	Form 2	Form 3	Form 4	Form 5
call	called	called	calls	calling
fix	fixed	fixed	fixes	fixing

❻ The verb *be* has eight forms, so it does not fit neatly into the table below.

Form 1	Form 2	Form 3	Form 4	Form 5
am/are/be	was/were	been	is	being

---
[1] *Has* and *is* are the only irregular Form 4 verbs.

Activity 1   *Test Yourself!*

Step 1: Complete the following chart. If you have any problems with the spelling of regular verb forms, you should review Appendix B, beginning on page 136.

Regular Verbs

Example: *visit*

Form 1	Form 2	Form 3	Form 4	Form 5
visit	*visited*	*visited*	*visits*	*visiting*
1. call	called	called	calls	calling
2. happen				
3.			permits	
4. fix				
5.			dies	
6.				smiling
7.			marries	

Step 2: Complete the following chart. If you have any problems with Forms 2 and 3 of the irregular verbs, review Appendix A, beginning on page 133. If you have any problems with Forms 4 and 5, review Appendix B, beginning on page 136.

Irregular Verbs

Example: *eat*

Form 1	Form 2	Form 3	Form 4	Form 5
eat	*ate*	*eaten*	*eats*	*eating*
1.	drove			
2.	fell			
3.		felt		
4.	got			
5.				having
6.			pays	
7.		shot		

Activity 2   *Use It!*

Bring a newspaper to class. On the front page, underline two examples of each verb form, that is, two examples of Form 1, two of Form 2, etc.

 # Lesson 2

What Can Follow What

Points to Remember: Main Verbs and Auxiliary Verbs ·······················

❶ The last verb in a verb phrase is the main verb. All other verbs are auxiliary verbs[1] (or helping verbs).

           aux aux   main
a. Madame Vista <u>has been telling</u> fortunes for years.

            main
b. The captain <u>runs</u> the ship.

❷ The first verb of every verb phrase must agree in number with its subject.

       S   **V**
a. Most <u>cruise ships</u> <u>are</u> owned by large companies.
      plural   **plural**

       S   **V**
b. <u>Madame Vista</u> <u>predicts</u> the future.
     singular   **singular**

Activity 3   *Test Yourself!*

Underline the auxiliary verb(s) in each sentence. Circle the main verb.

    Example: *Pearl and a friend <u>are</u>* (*playing*) *tennis.*

1. Lonnie will not be calling Burl for a while.
2. Pearl hasn't seen her brother since January.
3. Ronny wasn't doing anything special at the time of the phone call.
4. Burl should not have committed the crime.
5. What would you have done?
6. Ronny is being blackmailed.

Points to Remember: Seven Rules of Verb Phrase Structure ··················

❶ After the verb *be*, you can use Form 3 or Form 5.

---

[1] The first auxiliary verb in any verb phrase is the power word. (See Chapter 2.)

24

a. Pearl <u>was shot</u> by Burl. **be** **3**

b. Pearl has <u>been getting</u> stronger for several months. **be** **5**

Be careful! Form 3 after *be* is passive. Form 5 after *be* is progressive.[1]

❷ After the auxiliary verbs *do*, *does*, and *did* you can use only Form 1.

Fast cars <u>do not help</u> the environment. **1**

❸ After *have*, *has*, or *had*, you can use only Form 3.

Many attack victims <u>have improved</u> their condition through sports. **3**

❹ After any modal, you can use only Form 1.

Burl <u>may win</u> the match next month. **1**

❺ A main verb in Form 2 or Form 4 always stands alone. You can never use a helping verb with a main verb in Form 2 or 4.

a. Lonnie <u>started</u> to blackmail Ronny last year. (Simple past tense) **2**

b. Madame Vista <u>advises</u> many people in Appleton. (Simple present tense) **4**

❻ A verb after a preposition must be in Form 5, the verb-*ing* form.

Burl won third prize in the match <u>without practicing</u> much before. **prep** **5**

❼ After the word *to*, you can usually use Form 1.

a. Ronny wants to <u>improve</u> his life. **1**

Be careful! The word *to* is sometimes a preposition. In that case, you must use Form 5.

b. Lonnie is looking forward <u>to having</u> breakfast in New York. **prep** **5**

Summary of What Can Follow What

do
does } + Form 1
did

is, are, am
was, were } + { Form 3
been, be   Form 5

may, might
could, can
will } + Form 1
ought to, should
etc.

have, has, had
being [2] } + Form 3

• Preposition + Form 5
• Main verbs in Form 2 and 4 always stand alone.

---

[1] Passive verbs will be covered in Chapter 5. Progressive Tenses will be covered in Chapter 4.

[2] *Being* cannot be followed by form 5 because there is no double progressive. **Wrong:** *He is being working.*

Activity 4   *Practice It!*

Choose the best verb for each blank and put it in the correct form. Write only one word in each blank.

Mr. Finster owns a Shelby Cobra, one of the great American sportscars. The Cobra was produced from 1962 to 1968. This car went from 0 to 60 miles per hour in 3.8 seconds and had a maximum speed of 162 miles per hour.

In the early 1950s, the best sports cars were being (build, spend) _____built_____ by

Europeans. One American, Carroll Hall Shelby, thought he could (build, do) _____ a
                                                                              1

fine American sports car by (put, separate) _____ an American V8 engine onto a
                                                         2

European chassis.[1] The car would (be, have) _____ a two–seat cockpit [2] and a long
                                                        3

hood. After (be, have) _____ rejected by General Motors, Shelby (drive, take)
                              4

_____ his ideas to Ford. The people there were very (excite, bore) _____
        5   6

by Shelby's ideas, and started to (play, work) _____ with him immediately.·
                                                        7

At first, the factory (produce, repair) _____ only one *Cobra*. That one car was
                                                8

(clean, paint) _____ many times, first one color, then another. Each time, it was
                      9

(build, test) _____ on the road and (photograph, solve) _____. It was
                    10   11

(become, see) _____ on several magazine covers.
                    12

Vocabulary

[1] a chassis: the frame that holds the car together
[2] a cockpit: the part of the car where the driver sits

26

When car lovers (become, see) _____ the car, many (earn, want)
                                         13

_____ to buy it. Of course, they (believe, adjust) _____ that a different
        14   15

car was on each magazine cover. They (doubt, think) _____ that the car was being
                                                                 16

(produce, win) _____ in large numbers. In fact, that would never (happen, travel)
                        17

_____. Shelby was constantly (buy, think) _____ of improvements for
        18   19

the Cobra. He didn't (delay, want) _____ to wait a long time before (refuse, try)
                                            20

_____ out his new ideas, so the factory just (build, fix) _____ the new
        21   22

ideas into the next car on the line.[1] As a result, no two Cobras were alike!

Points to Remember: Checking Verb Phrases From Right to Left ··············

1 If you check your verb phrases, you can avoid many common errors.

2 After writing a sentence, underline each verb phrase. Number every verb form. Label
modals "M" and prepositions "P."

         M   1   3   5
Burl should have been practicing the week before the match.

3 Start on the right. Look at each verb form and ask yourself if it can follow
the word to its left.

Correct example:

         M   1   3   5
Burl should have been practicing.

      OK   OK   OK   OK

1. *practicing*: Form 5 after *be*: OK!
2. *been*: Form 3 after *have*: OK!
3. *have*: Form 1 after a modal: OK!
4. *should*: agrees with *Burl*: OK!

Vocabulary
_____
[1] the line: the assembly line in the factory

Correct example:

Before being injured in an attack, Pearl rarely played tennis.

1. *injured*: Form 3 after *be*: OK!
2. *being*: Form 5 after a preposition: OK!

Wrong example:

Lonnie could not drove a car three years ago.

1. *drove*: Form 2 after a modal: **Wrong!**
2. *could*: Agrees with *Lonnie*: OK!

❹ The word order is different in questions. Therefore, you need to start on the left. Ask yourself if the auxiliary verb agrees in number with its subject to its right. Then look at the verbs on the right. Ask yourself if each verb form can follow the other verb form(s) to its left.

Correct example:

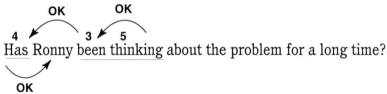

Has Ronny been thinking about the problem for a long time?

1. *has*: Agrees with *Ronny*: OK!
2. *thinking*: Form 5 after *be*: OK!
3. *been*: Form 3 after *have*: OK!

Wrong example:

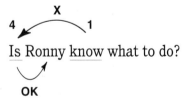

Is Ronny know what to do?

1. *is*: Form 4 agrees with *Ronny*: OK!
2. *know*: Form 1 after *be*: **Wrong!**

Activity 5   *Practice It!*

Follow the steps above to check each verb phrase. If the verb phrase is not possible in English, change it.

Examples:

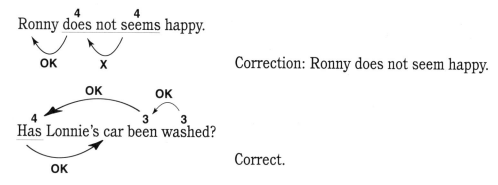

Correction: Ronny does not seem happy.

Correct.

1. Lonnie is looks pretty.
2. Lonnie can drives very fast.
3. The animals is being watched at the moment.
4. Lonnie received a lot of money without doing any work. (2 verb phrases)
5. The engine had been running all winter long.
6. Madame Vista had never been consulted by Ronny before.
7. Did Euclid invent the triangle?
8. Burl might had been playing ping-pong on the cruise ship.
9. Will those players come to the game?
10. Pearl play a lot of tennis.

Activity 6   *Use It!*

Step 1: Ask one or more native speakers the following questions and tape record their answers. (**Note:** Be sure your cassette fits your teacher's machine.)

1. Tell me about your present job or studies. Please give details like responsibilities, likes and dislikes, and plans for the future.

2. What is your opinion about the gun laws in this country? Please mention problems and solutions.

3. How would your life have been different if you had been born in 1776?

Step 2: Write down at least ten sentences from the interview. Each sentence must have a different verb structure. Label all verb forms, modals, and prepositions. Draw arrows to show that the verb phrases are correct.

Activity 7   *Use It!*

Find at least ten different verb structures in a magazine or newspaper. Copy the sentences and label all verb forms, modals, and prepositions. Draw arrows to show that the verb phrases are correct.

Activity 8   *Use It!*

Write a conversation of at least 200 words related to the story "Ronny's Mistake." The conversation can be between any two characters in the story—for example, between Lonnie and Ronny. Or it can be between any one character in the story and anybody else. Some possibilities: Pearl and her mother, or Lonnie and her car dealer. When you finish, underline all verb phrases. Label all verb forms, modals, and prepositions. Draw arrows to show that the verb phrases are correct.

Chapter 4

THE SIMPLE AND PROGRESSIVE TENSES

 Lesson 1

Time Focuses

Point to Remember: Three Focuses–Past, Present, Future ··················

Sixteen verb tenses are presented in this book! What a headache! However, there are only three *focuses:* past, present, and future. In speaking and writing, you must know when the focus is, and you must decide whether each verb is before, at, or after it.

Activity 1   *Study It!*

Imagine that the picture of Lonnie below is a flash photo taken at exactly 3:18:25 P.M. on May 7 of last year. That moment was the focus. This is an example of a *past focus.*

       at the focus
This picture <u>was taken</u> at 3:18:25 P.M. on

        at the focus
May 7 of last year. Lonnie <u>was holding</u> the

      before the focus
telephone. She <u>had just picked</u> it up and

     after the focus
<u>was going to call</u> Ronny.

Activity 2   *Analyze It!*

Decide whether each verb is *before, at,* or *after* the focus: 3:18:25 P.M. on May 7 of last year. Write *before, at* or *after* above each verb.

      at
  Lonnie (1) **felt** a little nervous. A few days before, Burl (2) **had told** her about Ronny's

plan to get rid of Pearl, and Lonnie (3) **had been thinking** about blackmail ever since. Lonnie,

who (4) **had never had** more than $100 in her bank account, (5) **was going to get** rich with

her knowledge.

Activity 3   *Study It!*

Imagine that the picture is a flash photo of Pearl right now, at this exact moment. The focus is *now*. This is an example of a present focus.

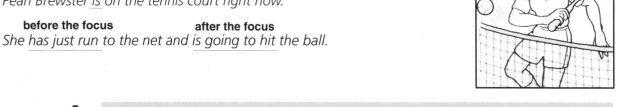

at the focus
Pearl Brewster <u>is</u> on the tennis court right now.

before the focus   **after the focus**
She <u>has just run</u> to the net and <u>is going to hit</u> the ball.

Activity 4   *Analyze It!*

Decide whether each verb is *before*, *at*, or *after* the present focus.

> **before**
She (1) **has been playing** for about an hour. She (2) **feels** good because she (3) **has gotten** much stronger since the attack. She (4) **is playing** hard. (5) She **is going to be playing** for about twenty more minutes. Because she (6) **feels** hot, she (7) **is going to go** for a swim after the match.

Activity 5   *Study It!*

Imagine that you have a time-camera that can take a picture of somebody in the future. The flash photo below will be taken at exactly 7:35:03 A.M. tomorrow. This is an example of a *future* focus.

at the focus
If all goes well, Lonnie <u>will be eating</u> breakfast at the Waldorf-Astoria

at the focus
at 7:35:03 A.M. tomorrow. She <u>is going to be</u> tired because she

before the focus
<u>will have driven</u> hundreds of miles during the night.

Activity 6   *Analyze It!*

Decide whether each verb is *before*, *at*, or *after* the focus: 7:35:03 A.M. tomorrow.

> **before**
She (1) **will not have slept** at all. Waiters (2) **will be bringing** her her favorite breakfast foods. She (3) **is going to have** chilled grapefruit, waffles covered with fresh strawberries, and strong coffee with real cream.

Points to Remember: The All-Time Non-Focus ·····························

① In addition to the three focuses, there is a non-focus, the all-time tense.[1]

Ships sail the seven seas. They carry goods and passengers. Most passengers travel for pleasure and business, but some passengers, like Burl, travel in order to hide.

② The all-time non-focus is used to present general truths, things that were true in the past, are true in the present, and will be true in the future.

> all-time non-focus = past + present + future

Activity 7   *Practice It!*

Choose the best verb for each blank in the general statements about crime and criminals. Put the verb in the correct form of the all-time tense. (**Note:** Put a power word in the box in number 5.) When you finish, discuss the statements with your classmates. Which ones do you agree with? Why?

Example:

People who (be, have) _____have_____ enough money ⟨ do ⟩ *not (believe, commit) _____commit_____ crimes.*

1. People (become, begin) _____ criminals because they (be, have) _____ unhappy.

2. Some people (be, have) _____ born criminals. There (be, have) _____ no way for them to become good people.

3. Burls says: "People who (be, have) _____ too nice never (come, see) _____ out on top."

4. Ronny says: "Countries that (reward, punish) _____ criminals severely can reduce crime."

Activity 8   *Analyze It!*

The focus can change in a paragraph. The paragraph below has three focuses. The first, May 5, has been labeled for you as an example. Find the other two.

first focus

Pearl was shot on <u>May 5 of last year</u>. She had been injured only twice before. At the age of eight, she fell out of a tree and broke her arm. She had been trying to see a bird's nest. As a result of that accident, her arm would be in a cast for weeks. Nine years later, when she was seventeen, she was in a car accident. She had gone to the beach, and a friend was driving her home in heavy traffic. Her friend hit another car, and Pearl, who had not been wearing a seat belt, hit her head on the dashboard.

---

[1] The traditional name for this tense is the *simple present tense*.

Lesson 2

The Uses of the Simple and Progressive Tenses

Points to Remember: Simple and Progressive Tenses ······················

❶ **Progressive tenses** indicate an action in progress at a certain time.

   a. **Progressive past:**   Pearl **was zooming** toward a bright light at 9:26 P.M. on May 5 of last year.

   b. **Progressive present:**   Pearl **is playing** tennis right now.

   c. **Progressive future:**   Lonnie $\left\{\begin{array}{c}\textbf{will} \\ \textbf{is going to}\end{array}\right\}$ be sitting in the hotel dining room at 7:35:03 tomorrow morning.

Adding the words *in the middle of* to these verb phrases does not change the meaning:

   d. Lonnie was (in the middle of) holding the phone at 3:18:15 P.M.

❷ The **simple tenses** can be used in several ways. The simple past and simple future are used to express one-time happenings.

   a. **Simple past:**   Pearl **met** a gentle man.

   b. **Simple future:**   Pearl $\left\{\begin{array}{c}\textbf{is going to} \\ \textbf{will}\end{array}\right\}$ **have** a pool party next Saturday.

❸ All three simple tenses are used to express conditions. In the examples below, *belong* refers to a condition, not an action.

   a. **Simple past:**   Years ago, the crystal ball **belonged** to Madame Vista's grandmother.

   b. **Simple present:**   Now, the crystal ball **belongs** to Madame Vista.

   c. **Simple future:**   In the year 2050, it **will belong** to Madame Vista's great-grandchild.

❹ The three simple tenses are used to express general truths or habitual actions.

   a. **Simple past:**   Fortune tellers often **found** themselves in prison in past centuries.

   b. **Simple present:**   Many people **consult** fortune tellers. (all-time tense)

   c. **Simple future:**   According to Madame Vista, people $\left\{\begin{array}{c}\textbf{will} \\ \textbf{are going to}\end{array}\right\}$ **consult** fortune tellers more in the future.

Activity 9 *Study It!*

Madame Vista, the fortune teller, believes that it is important to have discipline in one's daily life. For that reason, she follows a strict routine four days every week, Monday through Thursday. (She takes a three-day weekend.) Go over Madame Vista's daily routine with your teacher. Be sure you understand it. Your teacher can explain what a Ouija board is if none of the students in your class knows.

7:00 – 8:00 A.M.
gets up and makes breakfast

8:00 – 8:30 A.M.
showers and dresses

8:30 – 9:30 A.M.
meditates

9:30 – noon
does housework

noon 2:00 P.M.
has lunch with a friend

2:00 – 4:00 P.M.
receives clients

4:00 – 5:00 P.M.
walks

5:00 – 6:00 P.M.
makes dinner/family comes home

6:00 – 7:00 P.M.
has dinner

7:00 – 8:00 P.M.
uses a Ouija board with her husband

8:00 – 11:00 P.M.
does various things

This page may be reproduced for classroom use.

Activity 10 *Practice It!*

Work with a partner. Choose a time and ask your partner what Madame Vista is doing at that time. Your partner will answer based on the pictures on page 35. Then reverse roles.

Example:

Student 1: *It's 2:57 P.M. What is Madame Vista doing?*

Student 2: *She's receiving clients.*

Activity 11 *Practice It!*

Work with a partner. Ask your partner about Madame Vista at specific times last Tuesday or next Wednesday.

Possible questions: *Tell me about Madame Vista* $\left\{ \begin{array}{l} \textit{last Tuesday} \\ \textit{next Wednesday} \end{array} \right\}$ *at* _____ $\left\{ \begin{array}{l} \textit{A.M.} \\ \textit{P.M.} \end{array} \right\}$

Examples:

a. **Student 1:** *Tell me about Madame Vista last Tuesday at 9:37 A.M.*
   Student 2: *She was meditating.*

b. **Student 1:** *Tell me about her at 4:36 P.M. next Wednesday.*
   Student 2: *She will be walking.*

Activity 12 *Practice It!*

Ask your partner when Madame Vista does various things. (**Note:** Form 5 is used after *start* and *stop*. The infinitive can also be used after *start*.)

Examples:

a. **Student 1:** *What time does Madame Vista start* $\left\{ \begin{array}{l} \textit{meditating?} \\ \textit{to meditate?} \end{array} \right\}$
   Student 2: *She starts* $\left\{ \begin{array}{l} \textit{mediating} \\ \textit{to mediate} \end{array} \right\}$ *at 8:30 every morning.*

b. **Student 1:** *When does she meditate?*
   Student 2: *She meditates from 8:30 to 9:30 every morning.*

c. **Student 1:** *When does she stop meditating?*
   Student 2: *She stops meditating at 9:30.*

Activity 13 *Practice It!*

Read each paragraph and decide if its focus is past, present, future, or the all-time non-focus. Then choose the best verb for each blank, and put it in the correct tense. Put power words in the boxes. Use only these tenses: simple past, progressive past, simple present, progressive present, simple future, and progressive future. (**Note:** Put a power word in the boxes in 3 and 4.)

Examples:

Focus: past   present   ✓future   all-time

Tomorrow at 10:00 A.M., Pearl (start, hit) _____will start_____ to play tennis. She (catch, stop)_____will stop_____ playing tennis at noon. That means that at 10:36, she (play, throw)__will be playing__ .

1. **Focus:**   past   present   future   all-time

   Imre and his friends (spend, cost) _____ a lot of time watching the last Olympics. He (be, have) _____ especially interested in the Hungarian swimming team. Every time one of the Hungarian swimmers (lose, win) _____ a medal, Imre and his friends (stand, sit) _____ up and (speak, sing) _____ the Hungarian national anthem.

2. **Focus:**   past   present   future   all-time

   At 8:31 A.M. on June 8, 1988, Pearl and Ronny's father (eat, drink) _____ breakfast in his favorite restaurant. He (have, be) _____ retired at that time, but his wife (still / work, still/dance) _____, so he (often / spend, often / go) _____ out for breakfast. Unfortunately, he (usually / have, usually / cook) _____ fried eggs, sausage, fried potatoes, toast with lots of butter, and coffee with lots of cream.

3. **Focus:**   past   present   future   all-time

   A: Why [   ] the moon (look, earn) _____ big and round some nights, and small and crescent-shaped other nights?

37

B: This (have, be) _____ because of the way the moon (attach, reflect) _____ the sun's light. When the Earth (be, have)_____ between the moon and the sun, the moon (reflect, describe) _____ most of the sun's light to Earth. At those times, the moon (feel, look) _____ round, or full. When the Earth is not in that position, however, most of the reflected light (go, stay) _____ into space. The moon (reflect, appear) _____ crescent-shaped.

4. **Focus:**   past   present   future   all-time

   A: What [   ] you (do, make)[1] _____ next Friday night?

   B: I'm not sure. What do you have in mind?

   A: My roommate and I (have, make) _____ a party, and we hope you (have, be) _____ able to come.

Activity 14   *Use It!*

Step 1:   Practice the all-time tense by playing Twenty-Questions in two teams. Team One chooses a profession that almost all the team members know in English.

Step 2:   Team Two asks up to 20 general *yes/no* questions about the job.

Examples:

Does this person work with other people a lot?
Does this person design things?

Step 3:   When the members of Team Two agree that they know the profession that Team One is thinking of, they may ask one, and only one, specific question.

Example:

Are you thinking of a doctor?

Step 4:   If the answer to Team Two's direct question is "yes," Team Two scores a point. If the answer is "no," Team One scores a point. In either case, Team Two now thinks of a profession and Team One tries to guess it by asking 20 questions.

---

[1] When we are talking about something we are planning or preparing to do, we usually use *be going to* instead of *will.*

Activity 15 *Use It!*

Madame Vista is looking into her crystal ball. She sees these pictures of what some people are doing right now. Unfortunately, she's having a bad day, and parts of the pictures are hidden by large black splotches. What do you think the people in the pictures are doing? Why?

1

2

3

Activity 16 *Use It!*

Step 1: Use your knowledge and imagination to describe the daily routine of an interesting person—real or fictional. (Some possibilities: a sports or movie star, a super hero, a religious leader, a military officer.) Write that person's daily schedule.

Example:

Advisor to the President of the United States.

Time	Activity
7:00 – 8:00 A.M.	gets up and calls the president

Step 2: Make a copy of the routine, but omit the times.

Example:

Advisor to the President of the United States.

Time	Activity
	gets up and calls the president

Step 3: Give the copy of the schedule to a classmate. He/she will ask you questions like those in Activity 11 and fill in the times.

Step 4: Keep your daily schedules. You will need them later.

Activity 17 *Use It!*

Interview a classmate who comes from a place where life is different from your own. Find out about what people do in the different seasons there. Ask questions about sports, agriculture, religion, the arts, holidays, government, etc. Use the simple present tense (the all-time non-focus) to write at least five sentences about people's activities in different months and seasons.

Examples:

1. *In November, people in Canada begin shopping for Christmas.*
2. *In the beginning of the rainy season in Chad, the farmers begin to plant crops.*

Activity 18 *Use It!*

Ask a classmate about his/her favorite holiday. Give the name of the holiday. Then write at least five sentences about people's activities at different times during the day. Use the simple present tense (the all-time non-focus) and time expressions like *in the morning, in the afternoon, around 3:00 o'clock*, etc.

Example:

Mark's favorite holiday is Christmas.
1. *In the morning, families get up early, and everybody opens presents.*

Activity **19** *Use It!*

Step 1: Interview a classmate who is pretending to be a VIP (Very Important Person), perhaps the same person whose daily schedule he/she made in Activity 15. Questions should be about past events and future plans in the VIP's life. Use questions such as:

For the Past

When were you...?

When did you...?

When was the last time you...?

For the Future

When will you...?

When do you expect to...?

When do you plan to...?

Example:

Student 1: *When did you make your last movie?*
Student 2: *I made it two months ago.*

Step 2: Write an introductory sentence. Then write five past and five future sentences about the VIP.

Example:

I interviewed Laura Pelson, the film star.

1. Ms. Pelson made her last movie two months ago.

 Lesson 3

Non-Progressive Verbs: No Progressive Tenses

Points to Remember: Simple Tenses with Non-Progressive Verbs ··············

❶ Usually, simple tenses express habitual actions, and progressive tenses indicate happenings in progress.

a. **Habitual:** Lonnie **drives** her car almost every day.

b. **Now:** Lonnie **is driving** her car now.

c. **Habitual:** Mr. Brewster[1] often **ate** eggs and sausage for breakfast.

d. **8:17 one day:** At 8:17 on March 3, 1989, Mr. Brewster **was eating** eggs and sausage in his favorite restaurant.

---

[1] Mr. Brewster, the father of Ronny and Pearl Brewster, died three years ago.

② **Non-progressive verbs**, however, are not usually used in the progressive tenses. We usually use the simple tenses instead.

Habitual

a. Burl always **wants** more money.

Now

b. He **wants** more money now.

Habitual

c. Mr. Brewster often **needed** change for the pop machine.

At 8:47 one day.

d. At 8:47 on March 3, 1989, he **needed** change for the pop machine.

We do not usually say
Burl is wanting more money.   *or*   Mr. Brewster was needing change.

③ Some common non-progressive verbs

believe	exist	like	recognize
belong	fit	love	remember
consist of	hate	mean	seem
contain	hear	need	sound
cost	imagine	owe	suppose
dare	include	own	understand
dislike	know	possess	want

Activity 20   *Practice It!*

Change the time indicator to *now* and put it at the end of each sentence. If the verb is a progressive verb, change it to the progressive present tense. If the verb is non-progressive, keep the simple present tense.

Examples:

Lonnie drives her car every day.　　　*Sports cars usually cost a lot.*
Lonnie is driving her car now.　　　　*Sports cars cost a lot now.*

1. Sam often borrows money from a friend.
2. The cruise price of $789 usually includes the cabin and all meals.
3. Burl often listens to the birds in the park.
4. He often hears a bird that he can't identify.
5. Lonnie's medicine cabinet usually contains aspirin.
6. Mrs. Finster takes aspirin several times a month.
7. The management of the ABC company usually seems interested in the welfare of its workers.
8. The company's president visits the departments every week.
9. Some tension usually exists between the workers and the management.
10. Burl's clothes sometimes don't fit him.

Points to Remember: Verbs That Can Be Progressive or Non-Progressive ·······

❶ Some verbs that are usually non-progressive verbs have special meanings when they are used in progressive tenses. For example, the verb *see* is usually a non-progressive verb:

Example of **see** as a non-progressive verb:
Lonnie **sees** the car in front of her.

When **see** is used in a progressive tense, it usually has a different meaning.

Example of **see** as a progressive verb:
Pearl **was seeing** a new guy last month. (She was dating a new guy.)

❷ Common verbs that can be both progressive and non-progressive:

	Progressive Examples	**Non-Progressive Examples**
feel	He *is feeling* the tomatoes. **Meaning:** He is touching them to see if they are ripe.	He *feels* sick today. **Meaning:** He has a headache, stomachache, etc.
have	She *is having* a baby. **Meaning:** The baby is coming into the world. They *are having* a good time. **Meaning:** They are enjoying themselves. They *are having* dinner (lunch, breakfast, a snack). **Meaning:** They are eating.	She *has* a baby. **Meaning:** The baby is with her; it is already born. They *have* a lot of money. **Meaning:** The money belongs to them.
look	Burl *is looking* at a tree. **Meaning:** He is using his eyes to sense the tree.	Pearl *looks* great these days. **Meaning:** She seems to be in great health.
smell	The child *is smelling* the flowers. **Meaning:** The child is using her nose to sense the flowers.	The flowers *smell* wonderful. **Meaning:** They have a wonderful fragrance.

see	Pearl *is seeing* a new man. **Meaning:** Pearl and the new man are going out on dates. Mrs. Finster *is seeing* a doctor. **Meaning:** She is consulting a doctor.	Pearl *sees* the tennis ball. **Meaning:** She senses the ball with her eyes.
taste	The cook *is tasting* the sauce. **Meaning:** She is putting a little in her mouth to check the flavor.	The sauce *tastes* wonderful. **Meaning:** The flavor is wonderful.
think	He *is thinking* about Lonnie. **Meaning:** Lonnie is on his mind.	She *thinks* her attacker was a criminal. **Meaning:** She believes this.
weigh	The nurse *is weighing* Pearl. **Meaning:** Pearl is on a scale.	Pearl *weighs* 115 pounds. **Meaning:** That is her weight.

Activity 21 *Practice It!*

Change the time indicator to *now* and put it at the end of each sentence. If the verb is a non-progressive verb, change it to the progressive present tense.

Examples:

Pearl plays tennis several times a week.
Pearl is playing tennis now.

Burl usually needs money.
He needs money now.

1. The woman calls her lawyer every day.
2. Ronny often hears the neighbor's dog.
3. Ronny often sees dust in his TV room. (Think of the meaning of "sees.")
4. Madame Vista sees clients almost every day. (Think of the meaning of "sees.")
5. Aeronautic engineers often experiment with light-weight materials.
6. The cook in that restaurant always tastes the soup.
7. Lonnie often owes people money.
8. A full practice usually consists of warm-up exercises, drills, and a game.
9. Every year, the ABC Company pays dividends to its stockholders.
10. Ronny often has a cheese sandwich for lunch.

Activity 22 *Practice It!*

Choose the best verb for each blank and put it in the correct tense. Put power words in the boxes. Use only the simple and progressive tenses presented in this chapter. Use the progressive tense when possible. (**Note:** Some items have more than one focus.)

Example:

Pearl and her friend Apryl took a long walk in the woods last week. They had walked about three miles, but neither of them had spoken for several minutes.

A: A penny for your thoughts.

P: Oh, I [am] *not really (think, expect)_____thinking_____ about anything.*

1. Pearl and Apryl's conversation continued:
   A: Come on, Pearl!

   P: Well, all right. I [   ] (work, think) _____ about the attack. I [   ] just not (understand, need) _____ why anybody would do it.

   A: Who [   ] you (try, believe) _____ did it, Pearl?

   P: Well, I [   ] not (have, play) _____ any enemies, so I (think, speak) _____ it must have been just some crazy man.

2. Did you see that woman a few minutes ago!? She (taste, sound) _____ all the different kinds of mayonnaise in the store!

3. D: Hello?
   J: Hello, Debbie? This is Jack.

   D: Oh, hi, Jack. Listen, we (care, have) _____ dinner right now. Can I (talk, call) _____ you back at about quarter to eight?

   J: Quarter to eight? Hmmm... I (watch, see) _____ "Nova" then. It (seem, be) _____ a special program on computers, and I [   ] not (have, want) _____ to miss any of it. How about 8:00?

   D: Great! Talk to you then!

   J: Okay, bye.

   D: Bye–bye.

4. The Cold War (enjoy, begin) _____ after the end of World War II. At that time, most people (believe, spend) _____ that the nations that had won the war would work together on major world problems. However, disagreements between the Soviet Union and the West (cause, prevent) _____ coöperation. The Soviet Union (work, rest) _____ to spread Communism to as many countries as possible. The Western countries, on the other hand, (save, try) _____ to stop Communism. The result (be, have) _____ a great deal of international tension. The Cold War (begin, end) _____ in the early 1990s, when the Soviet Union (collapse, grow) _____. After the end of the Cold War, the only major country which still (have, be) _____ a Communist government (have, be) _____ the People's Republic of China.

5. A: Watch carefully through your binoculars and tell me exactly what you (see, hear) _____. I'll take notes.

    B: I see a tall man. He (get, drive) _____ out of his car right now.

    A: (be, have) _____ he bald, or [   ] he (have, need) _____ a lot of hair?

    B: He's as bald as a bowling ball!

    A: That (have, be) _____ Ronny. What [   ] he (go, do) _____?

    B: He (make, hold) _____ an envelope in one hand, and he (walk, eat) _____ to another car in the parking lot.

    A: Who (be, seem) _____ in the other car?

    B: A big man.

    A: [   ] he (have, need) _____ a beard?

    B: Yes, he [   ]. A big beard.

    A: That's Burl. What (happen, go) _____ now?

    B: The bald man (write, give) _____ the bearded man the envelope.

    A: What's Burl doing?

    B: He [   ] just (sit, consist) _____ there in his car... Ronny (play, go) _____ back to his car now... Ronny (drive, swim) _____ away, but Burl [   ] not. Burl (seem, owe) _____ to be waiting until Ronny's out of sight... Burl (begin, start) _____ his car. He [   ] not (seem, belong) _____ to be in a hurry. Now he (drive, run) _____ away to the North.

    A: Good work! Thanks!

Activity 23   *Use It!*

Work with a partner. Imagine you are exploring an interesting place: an island, a planet, the inside of a pyramid, a sunken ship, an ancient city, a haunted house, etc. Your partner is in a different place, and you are communicating by two-way radio. For example, you might be exploring a planet and your partner might be another astronaut orbiting the planet in a spaceship. Describe what you see, hear, smell, feel, etc. Your partner asks questions. Write out your conversation. Use the simple present and progressive present tenses. When you finish, underline the non-progressive verbs.

 **Lesson 4**

When *and* While: *Short and Long Actions*

Point to Remember: Short Action Interrupting Long Action · · · · · · · · · · · · · · · · · ·

These are examples of sentences with a short action interrupting a long action.

short action   **long action**

a. Lonnie **called** Ronny while he **was talking** with a client.

b. **While** Ronny was talking with a client, Lonnie called him.

c. **When** Lonnie called Ronny, he was talking with a client.

d. Ronny was talking with a client **when** Lonnie called.

Activity 24   *Practice It!*

7:00 – 8:00 A.M.
gets up and makes breakfast

There were various interruptions in Madame Vista's routine last Thursday. For each interruption, write one sentence with *when* and one with *while*.

Example:

7:16 A.M.—doorbell/ ring

*The doorbell **rang** while Madame Vista **was making** breakfast.*
*Madame Vista **was making** breakfast when the doorbell **rang.***

8:00 – 8:30 A.M.
showers and dresses

8:30 – 9:30 A.M.
meditates

noon – 2:00 P.M.
has lunch with a friend

4:00 – 5:00 P.M.
walks

5:00 – 6:00 P.M.
makes dinner

1. 8:21 A.M.—telephone / ring
2. 8:48 A.M.—there / accident / front / house
3. 12:36 P.M.—cat / catch / bird
4. 4:12 P.M.—Madame Vista / trip / curb
5. 5:45 P.M.—husband / bring / flowers

Activity 25 *Use It!*

Step 1: Read the situation below.

Unable to sleep, Ronny got up very early last June 14 and turned on the TV. All the stations were covering a space launch. The countdown was technically perfect; however, there was some other excitement at Cape Canaveral that morning. It involved Brian Ortega, an astronaut, and Marlene Smith, the owner of a candy company.

Step 2: Work with a partner. Student 1 looks only at the pictures of Ortega's activities on page 49. Student 2 looks only at the pictures of Smith's activities on page 50. Ask your partner questions about the activities of his/her character. (**Note:** Some possible questions are given at the bottom of each page.)

Step 3: With your partner, write at least five sentences with *when* and *while*.

Example:

When Smith entered the space center, Ortega was still sleeping.
Ortega was sleeping while Smith was talking with her boss.

Brian Ortega's activities, the morning of June 14

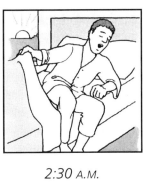

2:30 A.M.
got up

2:30 – 3:06
showered and dressed

3:06 – 4:00
breakfast

4:00 – 5:15
discussed mission

5:15
left dormitory

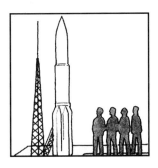

5:43
arrived at launch pad

5:45 – 6:00
talked with reporters

6:03
boarded space ship

6:05
began final
preparations for
countdown

7:32
countdown stopped

8:47
countdown resumed

8:57
blasted off

Possible questions about Smith:

What was Smith doing at 12:45 A.M? Did anything happen between two and three A.M?
What did Smith do after she changed her clothes?

49

Marlene Smith's activities, the morning of June 14

1:00 A.M.
got into van

1:00 – 2:14
drove to space center

2:14
entered space center as
reporter

2:17
changed clothes

2:20 – 5:15
hid in closet

5:15 – 5:29
snuck up to space ship

5:29 – 6:01
painted sign
on side of space ship

6:01 – 6:19
snuck back to closet

7:16
was discovered by
security officers

7:21 – 8:14
was questioned

8:15 – 8:46
was taken to jail

8:46
started sitting quietly

Possible questions about Ortega:

What was Ortega doing at 2:35 A.M? Did anything happen between three and four A.M? What did Ortega do after he left the dormitory?

Activity 26 *Use It!*

Use one or more items from each group below to interview a classmate. Write the answers in the third person (*he* or *she*). Write at least 100 words for each focus. All 100 words may be from one answer, or you may divide the 100 words among several answers. Use at least one time clause in each group.

Example:

Student 1 asks: *Where were you born?*
Student 2 answers: *I was born in a small town near Seoul, Korea.*
Student 1 writes: *Kim was born in a small town near Seoul, Korea.*

Past Focus

1. Describe your family at the time you were born.
2. Describe the neighborhood you lived in when you started going to school.
3. Tell me about a trick you or somebody you knew played when you were young.
4. Tell me about your favorite childhood toy or game.
5. Describe an interesting person in your family who is no longer alive.

All-Time Non-Focus

1. Describe the most exciting thing in your life right now (a hobby, a car, a relationship, etc.).
2. Describe the most interesting living person in your family.
3. Describe a pet that is alive now.
4. Describe your favorite room in your family's home. How does your family use that room?
5. Describe your favorite possession.

Future Focus

1. What will you do as soon as you get home tonight?
2. What will you be doing next Saturday at 9:30 P.M.?
3. If you are unmarried, describe your future spouse.
4. If you are studying far away from home, what will you do as soon as you get back to your hometown?
5. Describe your ideal future home.

Chapter 5

ACTIVE AND PASSIVE VOICES

 Lesson 1

The Concepts of Active and Passive

Activity 1 *Read It!*

Read the newspaper story below. It appeared in the *Appleton Daily News* the day after Pearl was attacked.

Appleton Daily News

 **Local Woman Shot Twice;
Few Clues to Help Police**

(*Appleton, May 6*) A local woman, Pearl Brewster, 28, was seriously injured in an attack at about 9:25 last night. Ms. Brewster was shot twice in her driveway as she was entering her home.

**Pearl Brewster:
Attack Victim**

She was rushed to Mercy Hospital, where she was operated on by a team of six doctors. The operation took six hours.

"It's amazing that she survived," said Dr. Maria Fernandez, a member of the operating team.

Almost no clues were left behind by the attacker.

Point to Remember: Passive Verb Phrases ·····························

Passive verb phrases usually consist of a form of *be* + Form 3 of the main verb. If a verb phrase is not passive, it is active.

Activity 2   *Analyze It!*

Underline each verb phrase in the article in Activity 1 and label it "active" or "passive." (**Note:** In the example below, *seriously* is an adverb, not a verb. Therefore, it is not underlined.)

Example:

                                                      passive
A local woman, Pearl Brewster, 28, <u>was</u> seriously <u>injured</u> in an attack. . .

Points to Remember: Agents and Subjects ·····························

1 Every sentence has a subject and an **agent**. The agent is the person or thing that does something. Active sentences tell what the agent does. In active sentences, the subject and the agent are the same.

    S
Lonnie is blackmailing Ronny.
  agent

2 Passive sentences tell what happens to the subject. The agent and the subject are different.

    S
<u>Ronny</u> is being blackmailed by Lonnie.
                       agent

3 The agent is usually not stated in passive sentences.

    S
<u>Ronny</u> is being blackmailed.

4 The three sentences above all describe the same situation, each in a different way.

Activity 3   *Practice It!*

Identify the agent in each sentence. It may or may not be stated. Then say whether the sentence is active or passive.

Examples:

People make millions of phone calls every day.
The agent is "people." The sentence is active.

Millions of phone calls are made every day.
The agent is "people." The agent is not stated. The sentence is passive.

1. Ronny (give) Burl a lot of money.
2. A lot of money (give) to Burl by Ronny.
3. A lot of money (give) to Burl.
4. The cook (add) eggs to the salad in a minute.

5. Eggs (add) to the salad a minute ago.
6. Thousands of cruises (take) every year.
7. People (take) thousands of cruises every year.
8. The farmers (milk) the cows in the morning and in the evening.
9. Truth, beauty, and goodness (study) by philosophers.
10. Last year's decrease in the price of gold (help) the jeweler.
11. Burl (win) third prize in the match last year.
12. Shipping companies (save) 7,900 miles by using the Panama Canal.
13. Ronny (become) scared when Madame Vista told him about his future.
14. A solution must (find) to all these problems!
15. Something wonderful (happen) to Pearl in April of last year.

Points to Remember: Why the Passive is Used ·····················

❶ The writer or speaker keeps the same subject in as many sentences as possible by mixing active and passive voices. The paragraph below is about the Cobra. The subject of most of the verb phrases is *Cobra*, *car*, or *it*.

> The automobile industry played a trick on car lovers with the Shelby Cobra, one of the great American sports cars. At first, only one Cobra was produced. That one car was painted again and again, each time a different color. Each time it changed color, it was tested on the road and photographed. The car appeared on several magazine covers. Most people believed that the Cobra was being produced in large numbers, and many decided they wanted to buy it.

❷ The subject is more important than the agent.
After the hot pepper was added to the soup, the child refused to eat it.

❸ The writer or speaker does not know the identity of the agent.
"Pearl has been shot!" Apryl told Jill.

❹ The action is the important thing. The agent is not important.
The Cobra was produced from 1962 to 1968.

❺ The writer or speaker wants to hide the identity of the agent. (See the cartoon).

Activity 4   *Analyze It!*

Look at each passive verb in the article about Pearl. Discuss which reason or reasons listed on page 54 explain why the passive is used in each case.

> *Example:*
>
> *was…injured: Reasons 1 and 3.*

Activity 5   *Practice It!*

Newspaper titles, or headlines, have a special grammar. For example, the headline on the article about Pearl was: **Local Woman Shot Twice**

When this headline is changed into a complete sentence, the result is: "A local woman was (or *has been*) shot twice." Here are some other headlines from last year's *Appleton Daily News*. Some are active and some are passive. Change each into a complete sentence.

1. Bridge Destroyed by Floods
2. Repairs Planned for City Hall
3. Governor to Visit Appleton
4. Appleton Defeats Polkville
5. Appleton Beaten by Newbury
6. Eldin County Wise in Ways of Recycling
7. New Courthouse OK'd
8. Mayor Opposes Tax Increase
9. Bank Robber Given 8 Years
10. Bookmobile Eliminated in Budget Cuts

Activity 6   *Use It!*

Underline examples of passive voice in the headlines and articles of a newspaper. If a headline uses special headline language, write an equivalent sentence above it.

 **Lesson 2**

Passive Structures in the Simple and Progressive Tenses

Points to Remember: Passive Structures ·······························

❶ The structure of a passive verb phrase is *be* Form 3. The verb *be* in the passive sentence is in the same tense as the main verb in the equivalent active sentence.

   a. Lonnie's car $\boxed{\text{is}}$ $\overset{3}{\textbf{driven}}$ hundreds of miles a week.

        $\boxed{\text{same tense}}$ (the simple present, all–time tense)

        Lonnie $\boxed{\textbf{drives}}$ her car hundreds of miles a week.

Other Simple and Progressive Tenses

Tense	Active	Passive
b. **Progressive Present**	Lonnie **is driving** her car.	The car **is being** driven.
c. **Simple Past**	Ronny **hired** Burl.	Burl **was** hired by Ronny.
d. **Progressive Past**	At 10:30 P.M., Pearl's doctors **were removing** the bullets.	At 10:30 P.M., the bullets **were being** removed.
e. **Simple Future**	The waiters **will serve** breakfast from six to nine tomorrow at the Waldorf-Astoria.	Breakfast **will be** served from six to nine tomorrow at the Waldorf–Astoria.
f. **Progressive Future**	At 7:30, the waiters **will be serving** breakfast.	At 7:30, breakfast **will be being** served.

Look at Appendix C on page 141 for examples of all the tenses in active and passive voices.

❷ Passive sentences include a **by phrase** when the agent is important.

    a. **Detective Kim:**   I agree that Burl could have shot Pearl, but I don't understand why he would have done it.

    Detective Sanders: Maybe he was paid by Ronny.

    The *by* phrase is usually omitted when it adds no useful information.

    b. Tennis is played by people in spring, summer, and fall.

    Only people play tennis, so the phrase *by people* is not useful.

❸ In speaking and in non-formal written language, the passive of many verbs can be formed with *get* + Form 3. This structure usually indicates either a sudden, unexpected action, or an action in which the subject changes condition (or both).

    a. **Less Formal:** Pearl never wants to get shot[3] again.

    b. **More Formal:** Pearl never wants to be shot[3] again.

You need to understand this structure when you hear it and read it. You do not need it in speaking and writing, however, because the passive with be is always correct.

Activity 7   *Practice It!*

Choose the best verb for each blank. Decide whether it should be active or passive, and put it in the tense indicated for its group. In each group, two are active, and two are passive. (**Note:** Put a power word in the box in number 9.)

Group 1: The Simple Present Tense

know   ✓score   pay   perform   make   ✓fall

Examples:

How many goals ___are scored___ *in an average game?*
A lot of rain ___falls___ *in the rain forest.*

1. People _____ millions of phone calls every day.
2. Thousands of dollars _____ to blackmailers every week.
3. Mozart's music _____ constantly.
4. The best cooks _____ how to prepare a large variety of foods.

Group 2: The Progressive Present Tense

transport   ✓operate   drive   listen   play

Example:

Around the world, doctors ___are operating___ *on dozens of patients right now.*

5. A red sports car _____ right now.
6. Thousands of people _____ to thousands of radios right now.
7. Pearl _____ tennis right now.
8. Goods of all kinds _____ at this very moment by trains, trucks, planes, and ships.

Group 3: The Simple Past Tense

make   understand   get   sweep   ✓teach

Example:

Lonnie ___was taught___ *to drive by her big brother.*

9. This room is dirty. It [_____] not _____ yesterday.
10. The weather _____ colder last week.
11. The movements of the pendulum _____ first by Galileo.
12. Pearl _____ a fantastic recovery in the weeks after her injury.

Group 4: The Future Tense

✓serve   ask   remove   put   throw

Example:

Lonnie ____will be served____ fresh, hot coffee in New York tomorrow morning.

13. Lonnie _____ some more gas in her car before long.
14. When the planes fly over the disaster area, packages of food
_____ _____ out.
15. Maybe Burl _____ Lonnie to marry him, maybe not.
16. During the operation, Mr. Wall's left lung _____.

Group 5: The Progressive Past Tense

unload   announce   ✓make   open   communicate

Example:

At 6:15 A.M. yesterday, coffee ____was being made____ in the hotel kitchen.

17. Randy was turning the doorknob. He _____ the door.
18. While the astronauts checked their instruments, engineers were making sure that the
NASA computers _____ with each other correctly.
19. The reporters had gathered at the White House; some important news
_____.

20. The truck had arrived at the back of the building, and the furniture
_____.

Group 6: With Modals

forgive   get out   fasten   ✓change   wash

Example:

Car owners should ____change____ their motor oil regularly.

21. Can you _____ white and colored clothes together in hot water?
22. Customers at self-service gas stations must _____ of their cars
before pumping gas.
23. Seat belts should _____ before the plane starts moving.
24. If Ronny tells Pearl what he did, he might _____.

Activity 8   *Use It!*

Work in groups of three or four. Think of several places near your school. Write down one sentence about something that is being done at each place. (For example, write "Cars are being repaired at the service station.") Then read your sentences out loud, but omit the location. The other students should guess the location.

Example:

Student 1:   *Cars are being repaired.*
Student 2:   *Are you talking about a service station?*

Activity 9   *Use It!*

Step 1:   Imagine a busy place like a bank, a bus station, a supermarket, a library, or a bowling alley. First, write the place you have chosen. Then write five passive sentences telling what is done there every day.

Example:

Every day at the bowling alley…

1. *Special shoes are worn.*

Step 2:   Imagine that same place at exactly 2:07 P.M. last Wednesday. Change your sentences to express what was happening at that moment.

Example:

At the bowling alley at 2:07 P.M. last Wednesday…

1. *Special shoes were being worn.*

 **Lesson 3**

Verbs that Cannot Be Passive

Points to Remember: Transitive and Intransitive Verbs •

❶ Verbs can be divided into two groups: **transitive** and **intransitive verbs**. Transitive verbs can take direct objects (d.o.) and can be passive.

Active Voice	**Passive Voice**
d.o.	
Lonnie is blackmailing <u>Ronny</u>.	Ronny is being blackmailed (by Lonnie).

❷ Intransitive verbs cannot take direct objects. Intransitive verbs cannot be passive.

a. Pearl has **arrived** at the tennis court. (no passive)

b. Ronny rarely **sleeps** well. (no passive)

❸ Some verbs can be transitive and intransitive.

a. **Intransitive:** My hands are **freezing**.

b. **Transitive:** He's **freezing** the chicken until next week.

❹ Other verbs can be both transitive and intransitive, but with different meanings.

a. **Intransitive:** Pearl has **run** to the net.

b. **Transitive:** The captain has been **running** the ship for years.

❺ The following verbs are almost always intransitive, but there may be some exceptions.

Some Common Intransitive Verbs

agree	come	grow up	rise
appear	consist	happen	seem
arrive	die	keep up	sit
be	exist	lie	snow
behave	fall	occur	stand
belong	go	rain	work

Activity 10   *Practice It!*

Change each sentence to the passive voice if possible. Omit the *by* phrase when the agent is obvious.

Examples:

Madame Vista is telling Ms. Wong's fortune.
Ms. Wong's fortune is being told by Madame Vista.

It is going to rain hard tonight.
(This sentence cannot be made passive.)

1. Somebody is calling Mr. Finster.
2. The judge agrees to reduce the fine.
3. The students have not learned that lesson.
4. Five major railways connect Beijing with other parts of China.
5. Peter Pan will never grow old.
6. Where are people hanging coats?
7. A grey coat is hanging on the hook near the door.
8. How do accidents happen?
9. Should teachers teach children to brush their teeth at school?
10. A water molecule consists of two hydrogen atoms and one oxygen atom.

Activity 11   *Practice It!*

Here is the end of the article about the attack on Pearl. Choose the best verb for each blank, and put it in the correct tense and voice. Use only the six simple and progressive tenses: the simple present, the progressive present, the simple past, the progressive past, the simple future, and the progressive future.

Ms. Brewster (plan, report) ___was reported___ this morning to be in poor condition. Two shots

(believe, hear) _____ at about 9:25 P.M. The shots (follow, result) _____
                    2   3

by the sound of a car taking off suddenly. Nothing (injure, see) _____ by any of the
                                                                        4

neighbors.

As of today, the Appleton Police Department (be, have) _____ no clues other than
                                                              5

the two 45 caliber bullets that (insert, remove) _____ from Ms. Brewster's chest.
                                                        6

Early this morning, police officers (move, study) _____ some tire tracks[1] in front of
                                                          7

Ms. Brewster's house, but they (learn, present) _____ nothing from them. "You
                                                        8

(keep, omit) _____ informed of any future developments," Chief Inspector Wes
                  9

McCloud told reporters. "Right now, we (baffle,[2] describe) _____ by this case, but we
                                                                    10

(not/defeat, not/heal) _____ . We are sure that this case (confuse, solve)
                              11

_____ soon."
      12

Neighbors say that Ms. Brewster (be, have) _____ a pleasant young woman who
                                                    13

often (invite, lose) _____ neighborhood children into her home for cookies. She
                          14

(drive, live) _____ alone.
                    15

Vocabulary

[1] tire tracks: marks that a car leaves on the road when it leaves quickly
[2] to baffle: to confuse

Until recently, Ms. Brewster (employ, fire) _____ as a teller by the National Bank.

16

The Daily News has learned that Ms. Brewster's uncle, Oswald Perkins, of Eugene, Texas, (die,

live) _____ recently and left Ms. Brewster a large sum of money. This (happen,

17

observe) _____ on April 27. The police cannot say if last night's attack (link, reverse)

18

_____ in any way to Ms. Brewster's inheritance. They say that

19

everything (now/investigate, now/forget) _____ .

20

Activity 12   *Use It!*

Step 1: The steps of an experiment are more important than the people performing them.
Therefore, the passive voice without *by phrases* is often used in laboratory reports. First read
the procedure. Then watch as the experiment is performed. Finally, write up a report using
the passive where appropriate. Your report will have three sections: the Procedure, the
Results, and the Explanation of the Results.

The Procedure

1. Assemble the following materials: a glass pie pan, a short candle, a glass at least two
inches (5.08 cm.) taller than the candle, about
two cups of water in a separate container, some
food coloring, and matches.
2. Light the candle.
3. Allow several drops of wax to fall into the middle
of the bowl.
4. Blow out the candle immediately.
5. Place the candle immediately in an upright
position in the middle of the bowl. Allow the wax
to cool.
6. Pour an inch (2.54 cm.) of water into the bowl.
7. Add three drops of coloring.
8. Relight the candle.
9. Cover the candle with the glass. (Figure 1)
10. Observe and record the results.

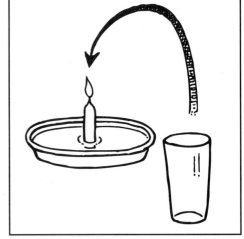

Figure 1

Step 2: Write up the procedure in one paragraph. Use the passive voice where appropriate. Begin
like the example on the next page.

The Procedure

The following materials were assembled: a glass pie pan, a short candle, a glass at least two inches (5.08 cm.) taller than the candle, about two cups of water in a separate container, some food coloring, and matches. The candle was lit, and several. . .

Step 3: Write up the *observable results. Observable results* means only what you saw. Do not give reasons for the results. You will do that in Step 4. (**Note:** Use the passive voice only where appropriate. You will not be able to use the passive voice in every sentence.) Here is some vocabulary:

flicker   go out   rise   smoke

Step 4: Explain the results. Use the passive voice only where appropriate. Here is some vocabulary:

burn up   equalize   high/low pressure   push

Activity 13   *Use It!*

A mysterious crime was committed last Friday. The criminal is unknown. You are a journalist for the local weekly newspaper, and your job is to write the article for tomorrow's newspaper. Write a report of at least 150 words. Use the passive voice where appropriate. Here are some possible crimes:

arson   kidnapping   a spy crime
a computer crime   poaching   a car theft

Chapter 6

THE BIG RIVER MIX-UP
LEARNING THE STORY

Activity 1   *Get the Background!*

Look at the story square on page 65. Then read this introduction.

The title of the second story in this book is "The Big River Mix-Up." It is about a scandal in big business and politics.

There are three people in this story. Justin and Betty live in Chicago and work at the national headquarters of the Unified Energy Company (UEC). Patty is a politician living in the state of Montana, in the Northwest of the United States. The fourth "character" in this story is not a person; it's a place, the beautiful Big River Valley in Montana.

You and your classmates are detectives, as you were in Chapter 1.

The story began thirty-seven years ago with a plane crash (Pictures 1 and 3). Today is election day in Montana, and the people of Montana will decide the end of the story.

As in the story "Ronny's Mistake," there are connections between the characters in the story. Your job is again to discover the connections.

Activity 2   *Get More Facts!*

Read these major points about the story as you study the pictures.

Thirty-seven years ago:

Picture 1:   Betty was about two years old. Her father was piloting a small plane when it crashed. Betty survived, but her mother and father both died in the crash. Betty stayed inside the plane and was rescued shortly.

Picture 2:   Justin's father took him to visit Wall Street. Justin was very excited and decided to spend his life in big business.

Picture 3:   Patty, also about two years old, was in a plane crash. Dazed,[1] she left the plane and followed a wolf into the forest.

Picture 4:   The Big River Valley in Montana was a beautiful wilderness[2] area where no people had ever lived or worked.

Ten years ago:

Picture 5:   Betty started working for UEC. Based in Chicago, this large company has energy interests in twelve states.

Picture 6:   Justin was becoming an important executive[3] in UEC. The Company's profits were rising.

Picture 7:   Patty was becoming an important environmentalist[4] in Montana.

Picture 8:   Big River Valley was the same as before.

Two months ago:

Picture 9:   During a romantic dinner, Betty learned of an opportunity to make a lot of money by helping the company.

Picture 10:   Justin assured the UEC Board[5] of Directors that a hydro-electric dam would be built on the Big River.

Picture 11:   Patty was running for governor.[6] She told a cheering crowd that as governor, she would not permit the dam to be built on the Big River.

Picture 12:   Big River was still the same as before.

Vocabulary

[1] dazed: very confused from a sudden shock
[2] wilderness: a natural area with no people living or working in it
[3] an executive: a manager with decision-making power in a company
[4] an environmentalist: somebody who works to protect nature
[5] a board: a committee
[6] a governor: the elected head of a state

One weekend a month ago:

Picture 13: After having her hair cut, Betty went to Las Vegas. The company had given her thousands of dollars. Her instructions were to talk with no one and to lose all the money, little by little.

Picture 14: Justin was pleased with an article in *The Capital News*.

Picture 15: The same weekend that Betty went to Las Vegas, Patty decided to take a break from the campaign.[1] Without telling anyone where she was going, she went camping alone.

Picture 16: Big River Valley was still the same as before.

Now: Today is election day. The voters of Montana are choosing their governor.
(**Note:** There are no pictures for *Now*.)

Next year:

Picture 17: Betty may be in jail, or she may be enjoying the money the company paid her after the Las Vegas trip.

Picture 18: Justin may be in jail, or he may be happily watching the rising profits of UEC.

Picture 19: Patty may be unemployed and living in a tent, or she may be the governor of Montana.

Picture 20: Big River Valley may be the same as before, or it may be the site[2] of a large hydro-electric dam.

Activity 3 *Discuss It!*

You have read some major points about the story, but there is still a lot you don't know. In small groups, discuss these questions.

1. What do you not know about the story?
2. Do you have any ideas about the links, or connections, between the characters?
3. What do you think you need to know to understand the story completely?

Vocabulary
[1] a campaign: a period of time when candidates present themselves to the voters
[2] a site: a location

Activity 4   *Learn the Whole Story!*

On a sheet of paper, write one or two *yes/no* questions that you can ask your teacher to learn more about Betty, Justin, and Patty. Ask your teacher your questions. Ask as many questions as you think you need to understand the story completely.

Examples:

Student 1:   *In Picture 7, was Patty famous?*
Teacher: *Not really famous, but many environmentalists knew her name.*

Student 2:   *In Picture 13, did anyone see Betty in Las Vegas?*
Teacher: *Many people saw her, but she talked with no one.*

Activity 5   *Double-Check It!*

Listen as your teacher reads each question. Then write the question and check (✔) the best answer.

Example:

Teacher: *How does Justin feel about Betty?*
Students write: *How does Justin feel about Betty?*

a. ☐ He loves her.
b. ☐ He's never met her.
c. ✔ It's not clear from the story.

1. _____

_____

a. ☐ They are cousins.
b. ☐ They are twin sisters.
c. ☐ They're unrelated.

2. _____

_____

a. ☐ In the airplane.
b. ☐ In Chicago.
c. ☐ In Las Vegas.

3. _____

_____

a. ☐ They forgot about each other.
b. ☐ They were both seriously injured.
c. ☐ It had no effect on them.

4. _____

_____

a. ☐ Betty helped her.
b. ☐ She was attacked by a wolf.
c. ☐ A wolf helped her.

5. _____

_____

  a. ☐ His family.
  b. ☐ Money.
  c. ☐ Sports.

7. _____

_____

  a. ☐ He wanted her to learn to gamble.
  b. ☐ He wanted her to win a lot of money.
  c. ☐ He wanted her to impersonate Patty.

9. _____

_____

  a. ☐ Voters would dislike a governor who gambled.
  b. ☐ Betty lost all the campaign's money.
  c. ☐ It didn't hurt her campaign; it helped it.

11. _____

_____

  a. ☐ Because she looks like Betty.
  b. ☐ Because he thinks she is not smart enough to govern.
  c. ☐ Because she will stop the dam project.

6. _____

_____

  a. ☐ To make money generating electricity.
  b. ☐ To protect the environment.
  c. ☐ To create a lake for water sports.

8. _____

_____

  a. ☐ So that she would look like Patty.
  b. ☐ She was tired of her old hairstyle.
  c. ☐ Justin didn't like her old hairstyle.

10. _____

_____

  a. ☐ Because nobody knew where she had gone that weekend.
  b. ☐ Because, in fact, she was in Las Vegas.
  c. ☐ Because she wants to be governor.

12. _____

_____

  a. ☐ It depends on the voters.
  b. ☐ Yes.
  c. ☐ Definitely not.

Chapter 7

THE BEFORE-FOCUS TENSES

 **Lesson 1**

The Progressive Before-Present Tense[1]

Points to Remember: The Concept of "Before-Focus" Tenses ·················

❶ **The Progressive Before-Past Tense**

Focus: two months ago

Betty **had been dating** Justin for about a month when he told her his plan to send her to Las Vegas.

$$= \left\{ \begin{array}{l} \text{Betty started dating Justin three months ago.} \\ + \\ \text{Justin told her about the plan two months ago.} \end{array} \right.$$

❷ **The Progressive Before-Present Tense**

Focus: right now

People **have been voting** in Montana since 6:00 A.M.

$$= \left\{ \begin{array}{l} \text{They are voting now.} \\ + \\ \text{The polls opened at 6:00 A.M.} \end{array} \right.$$

❸ **The Progressive Before-Future Tense**

Focus: tomorrow morning at 7:00.

By tomorrow at 7:00 A.M., election workers **will have been counting** the votes for ten hours.

$$= \left\{ \begin{array}{l} \text{They will begin counting at 9:00 tonight.} \\ + \\ \text{They will still be counting at 7:00 A.M. tomorrow.} \end{array} \right.$$

---

[1] The traditional name for this tense is the *present perfect progressive*.

Activity 1   *Practice It!*

First, decide which is the focus: past, present, or future. Then choose the verb, and put it in the best tense. Use only the three progressive before-focus tenses.

Example:

Focus: ✔*past*   *present*   *future*

Patty quit her job at the Montana Department of Natural Resources a year ago to run for governor. At that time, she (play, work) _____had been working_____ *in the same office for five years.*

1. **Focus:**   past   present   future

   A large group of students will take the TOEFL next Tuesday. The test will begin at 9:00 A.M. By 11:30, the students will be tired because they (concentrate, infuriate) _____ for two and a half hours.

2. **Focus:**   past   present   future

   Ellen has blond hair and blue eyes. Every spring, she tries to get a sun tan. An hour ago, I saw Ellen in front of her dorm. At that time, she (lay, lie) _____ in the sun for about a half an hour, and she was starting to turn pink.

3. **Focus:**   past   present   future

   Right now, Ellen is as red as a lobster. She (lay, lie) _____ in the sun for one and a half hours.

4. **Focus:**   past   present   future

   Ellen has to leave for an appointment an hour from now. I'm afraid her skin is going to be badly burned by that time unless she goes inside. By that time, she (lay, lie) _____ in the sun for two and a half hours.

5. **Focus:**   past   present   future

   Lewis and Clark (explore, shoot) _____ western North America for almost 19 months when they finally reached the Pacific Ocean on November 7, 1805.

Activity 2   *Study It!*

The pictures below show some things that are happening **right now**.

Active examples:

a. Patty **has been campaigning** for a year.

$=\begin{cases} \text{She is campaigning now.} \\ + \\ \text{She began campaigning a year ago.} \end{cases}$

b. Some animals **have been drinking** from the river for a few minutes.

$=\begin{cases} \text{They're drinking now.} \\ + \\ \text{They began drinking a few minutes ago.} \end{cases}$

Points to Remember: The Progressive Before-Present Tense · · · · · · · · · · · · · · · · ·

❶ We use the **progressive before-present tense** to indicate that an action began in the past and is still going on in the present. The power words for this tense are *have* and *has*. Contractions are *'s* and *'ve*.

    a. Patty has been campaigning.   ➤   Patty**'s** been campaigning.
    b. They have been drinking.   ➤   They**'ve** been drinking.

❷ This tense is rarely used in the passive voice.

❸ We use *for* and *since* to indicate **how long** an action has been going on.

For is followed by a length of time.

    a. Water has been flowing in the Big River for about two million years.

Since is followed by a word or phrase which indicates a point in time.

    b. Patty's popularity has been increasing **since last Wednesday**.

Since can also be followed by an event in the past tense.

    c. Patty's popularity has been increasing **since she explained everything on TV last Wednesday**.

4 We use *how long* to ask about duration.

Question:	How long has Justin been playing golf?
Possible answers:	For about an hour. *or* Since 8:00 A.M.
Other possible answers:	For thirty-two years. *or* Since high school.

Activity 3   *Practice It!*

Complete each expression with *for* or *since*.

Examples:

a month ———▶ *for a month*
last November ———▶ *since last November*

1. she returned from Las Vegas
2. five minutes
3. Tuesday
4. she quit her last job
5. two years

6. a few months
7. last week
8. their plane crashed
9. six o'clock
10. three days

Activity 4   *Practice It!*

In each item, make two sentences with the words given. The first sentence must be in the progressive present tense. The second sentence must be in the progressive before-present tense using the expression in brackets. Make your sentences true by using the names of real people, places, etc.

Example:

(Name) / teach / this school / (19__)
Miss Jackson is teaching in this school now. She has been teaching here since 1992.

1. My sister (or brother, uncle, etc.)/collect/stamps (or coins, etc.) / (19__)
2. I/live/(address) / [months or years]
3. I/wear/hair/long (or short, medium length, curly, etc.) / [months or years]
4. My uncle (or aunt, brother, etc.)/work/ (company) / (19__)
5. I/wear/ (clothing) / [hours, months, years]
6. (company)/manufacture/(product) / [months or years]
7. Mr. (name)/live/White House in Washington / (19__)
8. (Name)/rule/my country / (years)
9. I/study/English/(city) / (weeks or months)
10. I/breathe / (years)

Activity 5   *Use It!*

Step 1:   Work in groups of four. Student 1 reads her/his first sentence from any item in Activity 4 above. Student 2 asks Student 1 a question with *how long* about that sentence. Student 1 answers.

> *Example:*
>
> ***Student 1:***   *My brother is collecting coins.*
> ***Student 2:***   *How long has he been collecting them?*
> ***Student 1:***   *He's been collecting them since 1991.*

Step 2:   Student 3 asks Student 4 a related question, and Student 4 answers.

> *Example:*
>
> ***Student 3:***   *How long has Julien's brother been collecting coins?*
> ***Student 4:***   *He's been collecting them since 1991.*

Activity 6   *Use It!*

Choose five of the questions below. Walk around asking each question until you get a "yes" answer. When somebody answers "yes," ask about that topic with the words *how long*. Then write two sentences about that student, one with *for*, and one with *since*.

> *Example:*
>
> *Do you live in an apartment?*
>
> ***Sally:***   *Bert, do you live in an apartment?*
> ***Bert:***   *No, I don't.*
> ***Sally:***   *Jane, do you live in an apartment?*
> ***Jane:***   *Yes, I do.*
> ***Sally:***   *How long have you been living in an apartment, Jane?*
> ***Jane:***   *I've been living in an apartment for six months.*
> ***Sally writes:***   *Jane has been living in an apartment for six months.*
> *Jane has been living in an apartment since July.*

Questions to ask:

1. Do you sing?
2. Do you cook?
3. Do you drive?
4. Do you listen to (*kind of music*) ?
5. Do you eat hamburgers (spaghetti, kemchi, kabsa, tempura, beans, a lot of salad, etc.)?
6. Do you play soccer (poker, volleyball, badminton, tennis, etc.)?
7. Do you bowl (swim, hunt, camp, hike, dance, climb mountains, sail, etc.)?
8. Do you collect stamps (coins, postcards, fossils, autographs, CDs, clothes, etc.)?
9. Do you watch (*TV program*)?
10. Do you play the piano (trumpet, drums, guitar, etc.)?

◈ Lesson 2

The Before-Present Tense[1]

Activity 7   *Read It!*

Step 1:   Read part of Patty's last campaign speech, which she gave last night.

> Folks, I hope you agree that I'm the best candidate for governor of this state. I've worked in four different departments of the state government. I've gotten federal money[2] for the construction of new highways. I've improved conditions for our young people. I've developed plans for Montana businesses to sell their products outside the state. I've worked with miners[3] to bring new technologies to Montana. And, most recently, as Director of the Department of Natural Resources, I've struggled to protect our environment, from the plains in the East to the mountains in the West!

Step 2:   Find all the examples of the before-present tense in the paragraphs above. The before-present tense consists of *have* or *has* + Form 3.

Step 3:   Discuss these questions. What experiences has Patty had that would make her an effective governor? Can you tell from this speech **when** Patty got the federal money? Or **when** she developed plans for Montana business?

Points to Remember: The Before-Present Tense ·······························

❶ The before-present tense is used to express a past action that has happened (or not happened) before the present. The time of the action is not given. The time may be unknown or unimportant.

Active examples:

   a. Patty has worked at the Department of Commerce (DOC).
   b. Patty has never gambled in her life.

Passive examples:

   c. Thousands of votes have been cast in today's election.
   d. A dam has never been built on the Big River.

❷ The before-present tense is also used to express a repeated action in the past. This action may or may not be repeated in the future.

> Patty has given 936 speeches in her campaign.
> (Maybe she will give another today, election day.)

Vocabulary

---

[1] The traditional name for this tense is the *present perfect*.
[2] Federal money: money from the US government in Washington
[3] a miner: someone who digs valuable materials like gold or coal from the ground

❸ The before-present tense is also used to express an action or condition that began in the past and has continued until now.

> Patty has lived in Helena since the age of 22. (She still lives there now.)

❹ The before-present tense is also used to express a past action with present results. The time of the action is not given.

    a. **Past action:** Patty has worked in four different departments of the state government.
    Present result: She knows a lot about the government.

    b. **Past action:** Patty has arrived at a polling place in Helena.

    Present result: She is talking with people there now.

❺ These are examples of time expressions used with the before-present tense.

    a. **No time expression:** Patty has had a lot of experience in government.
    b. Betty has **recently** bought a lot of new things.
    c. Betty has bought a car and a television **in the last two weeks**.
    d. Thousands of people have voted **so far today**.

    e. **Question:** Have you ever voted in a national election?
    Answer: Yes, I have. Three times.

    f. Justin has played three holes on the golf course
$$\left\{\begin{array}{l}\text{so far.}\\ \text{now.}\\ \text{up to now.}\\ \text{until now.}\\ \text{as of now.}\end{array}\right.$$

The five choices in example f. all have the same meaning.

Activity 8   *Analyze It!*

Study the examples of the before-present tense and the simple past tense and answer the questions.

Before-Present	Simple Past
Example:	
Patty has worked in four different departments in the state government, including the Department of Commerce (DOC).	Hal Miller, the other candidate for governor, was a clerk at a hotel from the age of 18 to 23.
When did she work at the DOC?	When did Miller work as a clerk?
☐ Age 25 to 2. ☑ Impossible to say.	☑ Age 18 to 23. ☐ Impossible to say.

1. Patty has lived in Helena since the age of twenty-two. Where does she live now?

   ☐ Helena.
   ☐ Impossible to say.

2. Hal Miller lived in Billings for seven years. Does he live in Billings now?

   ☐ Yes.
   ☐ No.

3. Patty has arrived at one of the polling places[1] in Helena. Where is she now?

   ☐ At a polling place.
   ☐ Impossible to say.

4. Hal Miller arrived at a restaurant for breakfast at 7:23 A.M. today. Where is Miller now?

   ☐ At the restaurant.
   ☐ Impossible to say.

5. Patty has never gambled in her life. Is it possible for Patty to gamble in the future?

   ☐ Yes.
   ☐ No.

6. Patty's biological father[2] never gambled in his life. Is it possible for her biological father to gamble in the future?

   ☐ Yes.
   ☐ No.

Activity 9   *Practice It!*

Choose the best verb for each blank, and put it in the before-present tense or the simple past tense. (**Note:** Some verbs are passive.)

Example:

Patty (elect, visit) ____has visited____ 63 Montana cities in the last week. Last Tuesday, she (take, give) _____gave_____ speeches in eleven towns. Her voice (be, have) _____was_____ really weak by the end of that day!

1. A: Mary seems really upset with Karen.

   B: I don't blame her. Karen (borrow, buy) _____ Mary's new camera a week ago. Mary wants to take some pictures, but Karen still (not/buy, not/return) _____ it.

2. Justin (receive, manufacture) _____ three big promotions since 1992. The last one (be, have) _____ three weeks ago.

Vocabulary

[1] a polling place: a place where people vote
[2] biological father: her first father, not Leroy Flick, who is her adoptive father

3. A complete system of laws (concern, develop) _____ over several centuries by the ancient Romans. The laws (erupt, organize) _____ by Emperor Justinian I in the sixth century A.D. Since that time, the laws of most of Western Europe (consider, influence) _____ by Roman law.

4. Little Johnny really loves his new sunglasses. He (put, turn) _____ them on as soon as he (get up, turn around) _____ this morning. Since then, it (develop, get) _____ cloudy, but he (not/take, not/put) _____ them off.

Activity 10   *Practice It!*

Choose the best verb for each blank and put it in the correct tense. Put power words in the boxes.

1. The Delmarva Peninsula Fox Squirrel is an _endangered species_. This (mean, believe) _____ that this kind of squirrel is disappearing rapidly. Every year, there (have, be) _____ fewer and fewer of them. The major reason (be, have) _____ that, for the last few decades, more and more people (build, destroy) _____ their vacation homes on the sandy beaches of the Delmarva Peninsula, which (include, exclude) _____ most of the state of Delaware and parts of Maryland and Virginia. The fox squirrel (live, play) _____ in the sandy soil where people (hate, like) _____ to build their homes. When people (destroy, build) _____ their houses, they (build, destroy) _____ the homes of the fox squirrel. As a result, the fox squirrel (find, lose) _____ much of its natural habitat.

   People are continuing to build more and more homes on this land. ☐ the fox squirrel (be, have) _____ able to survive? Nobody (know, think) _____. The next few years (be, turn) _____ very important to the survival of this little animal.

2. Last Wednesday, Patty was interviewed on a Montana TV station. Here is part of the interview:

   I: Ms. Flick, thank you very much for being here with us tonight. A week ago, there (be, have) _____ a picture in *The Capital News*. It (show, see) _____ you gambling in Las Vegas, Nevada. You say you (not/be, not/have) _____ in Las Vegas at that time. You say you went camping.

   P: That's right. I don't know who the woman in Las Vegas (be, have) _____. It (not/be, not/have) _____ me. Whoever she was, she certainly (be, have) _____ a lot of money to lose! It (be, have) _____ true that I (come, go) _____ camping last weekend. I (come, go) _____ alone because I (not/dislike, want) _____ to be disturbed. I wanted a couple of days to think—with no campaign workers and no reporters.

I: [_____] you ever (gamble, calculate) _____ in your life?

P: No, I [_____] not. Let me say something more about that. I (never/gamble, never/camp) _____ in the past, and I promise the people of Montana that I (never/gamble, never/camp) _____ in the future. Furthermore, if anybody in the state of Montana has ever seen me gambling, I invite you now to speak up. I feel confident making this challenge because nobody (ever/see, ever/show) _____ me gambling.

Activity 11   *Use It!*

Step 1: The Desert Hotel in Nevada is owned by Ricardo Ortiz. He bought it fifteen years ago. Work with a partner. Student 1 looks only at the picture of the Desert Hotel 15 years ago on this page. Student 2 looks only at the picture of the Desert Hotel today on page 80. Discuss with your partner the differences in the pictures. (**Note:** You will use the past and present tenses in Step 1, not the before-present tense.)

Examples:

More palm trees have been planted.
Mr. Ortiz has built a casino in the last fifteen years.

Student 1:   Use these expressions to describe to your partner the hotel as it was 15 years ago:

In front of the hotel. . . To the left of the hotel. . . To the right of the hotel. . .
In front of the hotel. . . Behind the hotel. . . Fifteen years ago. . . In 19__. . .
There was. . . There were. . . The hotel had. . .

Use these expressions to ask your partner about the hotel today:

Is there a. . . ? Are there any. . . ? Does the hotel have. . . ? How many. . . ?
What shape. . . ? What color. . . ? Where. . . ?

Student 2: Use these expressions to ask your partner about the hotel as it was 15 years ago.

Was there a. . . ? Were there any. . . ? Did the hotel have. . . ? How many. . . ? What shape. . . ? What color. . . ? Where. . . ?

Use these expressions to describe the hotel to your partner.

In front of the hotel. . . To the left of the hotel. . . To the right of the hotel. . . On top of the hotel. . . In front of the hotel. . . Behind the hotel. . . There is. . . There are. . . The hotel has. . .

Step 2: With each of you still looking only at your own picture, write ten sentences together about changes at the Desert Hotel since Mr. Ortiz bought it. Sentences may be active or passive. Use the before-present tense.

Lesson 3

The Before-Past Tenses

Activity 12 *Study It!*

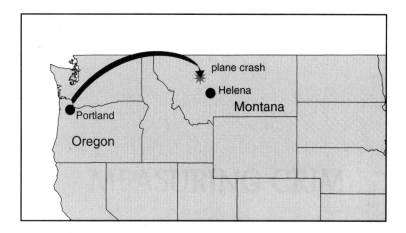

Patty's family **had been traveling** for 3 hours and 26 minutes when their plane crashed.

$$= \begin{cases} \text{They took off from an airport in Portland, Oregon at 10:30 A.M.} \\ + \\ \text{At 1:56 P.M., the plane crashed in Montana.} \end{cases}$$

Points to Remember: The Progressive Before-Past Tense[1] ·

❶ We use the **progressive before-past tense** to indicate that an action began in the past before another action in the past.

❷ The idea of **interruption** is often important with the **progressive before-past tense**. The power word for this tense is *had*. The contraction is *'d*.

They **had** been traveling.   They**'d** been traveling.

❸ This tense is rarely used in the passive.

---
[1] The traditional name for this tense is the *past perfect progressive.*

Activity 13 *Study It!*

Bobby Newton runs the roulette table where Betty lost $162,240 a few weeks ago. Bobby works in a wild city, but he has a strict personal routine. Here is what he does every work day. Go over Bobby's schedule. Make sure you understand it.

11:00 – noon

gets up and has
breakfast

noon – 12:30

takes a shower

12:30 – 1:30

practices Tai Chi

1:30 – 3:30

does various activities
and eats lunch

3:30 – 4:00

drives to work

4:00 – 8:00

deals blackjack

8:00 – 8:30

takes a supper break

8:30 – midnight

runs a roulette table

midnight – 2:00

exercises at the health club

2:00 – 4:00

relaxes and goes to bed

Activity 14   *Practice It!*

In each item, make a sentence about how long Bobby had been doing one thing when he was interrupted by something else on the day Betty came to Las Vegas.

Example:

12:50 P.M.—pager beeped
When his pager beeped, Bobby had been doing Tai Chi for 20 minutes.

1. 3:42 P.M.—saw an accident
2. 6:00 P.M.—took his first break
3. 8:17 P.M.—spilled ketchup on the floor
4. 8:32 P.M.—Betty started playing at his table
5. 8:34 P.M.—Betty lost her first $1,000
6. 9:21 P.M.—a photographer took a picture of Betty
7. 1:00 A.M.—Bobby started lifting weights
8. 2:17 A.M.—heard a siren outside
9. 3:12 A.M.—started reading
10. 3:23 A.M.—fell asleep in his chair

Points to Remember: The Before-Past Tense ·

❶ We use the **before-past tense** to indicate that one action in the past happened before another action in the past. The power word for this tense is *had*.

Active example:

a. $\left\{ \begin{array}{l} \text{By the time} \\ \text{When} \end{array} \right\}$ Betty left the casino, she **had lost** $162,240.

(by the time = not after)

Passive example:

b. By the time Betty left the casino, her picture **had** already **been published** in several Montana newspapers.

❷ This tense is often used in sentences with *by the time* and *when*. The verb in the before-past tense happened first. The verb in the simple past tense happened second.

a. **When** Patty **was rescued,** she **had spent three weeks** in the woods.

These same ideas can be expressed with *before* and *after*.

b. **Before** Patty was rescued she $\left\{ \begin{array}{l} \text{spent} \\ \text{had spent} \end{array} \right\}$ three weeks in the woods.

c. **After** Patty $\left\{ \begin{array}{l} \text{spent} \\ \text{had spent} \end{array} \right\}$ three weeks in the woods, she was rescued.

In b. and c., both the simple past and the before-past are correct.

Activity 15   *Practice It!*

Look at Bobby Newton's schedule on page 82. Your teacher will give you a specific time of day. What had Bobby already done by that time last Tuesday? Study the schedule for 30 seconds, then close your book, and say as many of his activities as you can remember.

Examples:

Teacher: 1:15 P.M.

> *By 1:15 P.M. last Tuesday, Bobby had already had breakfast.*
> *By 1:15 P.M. last Tuesday, Bobby had been practicing Tai Chi for 45 minutes.*

Activity 16   *Use It!*

Every time you come to a new school, you have new experiences. You do things that you have never done before. Write down one or two things that you had never done before coming to the school where you are studying now. Then read your sentences aloud. (**Note**: As you listen to your classmates' sentences, try to remember them. Your teacher may ask you to repeat them.)

Example:

> *Before I came to this school, I had never studied in a class with both men and women.*

Activity 17   *Read It!*

Read about the lives of two important men in the history of Montana. Then discuss the two men's lives and personalities. How were they similar? How were they different?

Marcus Daly (1841-1900): "The Copper King"

Marcus Daly was born in Ireland in 1841. As a young man, he emigrated to the United States. After some years in the mining business in California, he was sent by his company to Montana. A self-made man,[1] he had taught himself mine engineering. In hopes of making his fortune in silver, he bought a mine for $30,000 in 1880. Surprisingly, in addition to silver, he found vast[2] quantities of copper. He soon had his first million dollars.

Daly's mine became the world's largest producer of copper. Near the mine, Daly planned the town of Copperopolis, which later became Anaconda. He hoped that it would become the capital of the state. Daly became active in Montana politics and was often involved in political power struggles.[3]

Vocabulary

[1] a self–made man: a man who has educated himself
[2] vast: very, very large
[3] a power struggle: a fight for power

In Anaconda, he built the Marcus Daly hotel, one of the world's most magnificent hotels at the time. He also founded[1] the *Anaconda Standard* newspaper and equipped it with the most modern machinery of the day. Daly had many investments, including a horse ranch. At the time of his death, his fortune was estimated at $25,000,000.

Plenty Coups (1848-1932):
The Last Traditional Chief of the Crow Indians

When Plenty Coups[2] was born in 1848, more and more whites were coming west. They were taking the land and killing all the buffalo.[3] The Crow Indians had always depended on these animals for food, shelter, and clothing, and it was clear that they would have to learn a completely new way of life. By the age of thirty, Plenty Coups had become a chief in the traditional way: he had proven himself in battle. He realized, however, that the Crow traditions would not allow his people to survive in a changing Montana.

Plenty Coups learned as much as he could about white people. At his trading post,[4] he learned to do business with them. He made several trips to Washington D.C. on behalf of [5] the Crow. A very sociable man, he made many friends there. As a result, when there were problems on the reservation[6] between the native Americans[7] and the U.S. government, Plenty Coups was often able to get help from his friends in Washington.

Plenty Coups managed to get along[8] in two worlds. He became a Catholic, but also remained a member of the Crow religious organization. He participated in the Catholic Mass,[9] but also did the traditional Crow dances. He maintained close ties with friends and family, but also earned the friendship and respect of many whites. When he died, the Crow recognized him as their last traditional chief.

Vocabulary

[1] to found: to establish, to begin (a business)
[2] Plenty Coups: A coup is a success in battle. The name Plenty Coups, therefore, means "Many Successes in Battle" (The p in *Coup* is silent.)
[3] buffalo: animals similar to cows
[4] a trading post: a store where people could exchange or trade things
[5] on behalf of: representing
[6] a reservation: a special area assigned by the US government for Indians to live in
[7] native Americans: a modern term for American "Indians"
[8] to get along: to have some success
[9] Mass: a Catholic ritual, or ceremony

Activity 18 *Use It!*

Work with a partner. Student 1 covers page 87 and looks at this page. Student 2 turns to page 87.

Student 1: Complete the questions below by putting one word in each blank. Ask your partner the questions and write down the answers.

Example:

When _____was_____ Plenty Coups born?   Answer: _____1848_____

1. _____ happened _____ Plenty Coups _____ 1873?
2. When _____ Plenty Coups go to Washington D.C. _____ the first time?
3. What _____ he do on the reservation _____ 1883?
4. _____ happened _____ Crow children _____ 1884?
5. _____ happened _____ the Crow in 1887?
6. When _____ Plenty Coups become chief of all the Crow?
7. What _____ he do in Washington D.C. in 1921?
8. When _____ he die?

Student 1: Use this table to answer your partner's questions about Marcus Daly.

1841	Born in Ireland.
1857	Emigrated to the United States.
1876	Sent to Butte, Montana, by his company.
1880	Bought the Anaconda mine near Butte; started his own company, the Anaconda Company.
1883	Planned the town of Anaconda.
1887	Became a millionaire.
1888	Anaconda became a city.
1895	Daly's Anaconda Company became the world's largest producer of copper.
1900	Died.

Student 2: Cover page 86. Use this table to answer your partner's questions about Chief Plenty Coups.

1848	Born near Billings.
1873	Became the chief of the Mountain Crow Indians.
1880	Made his first trip to Washington, D.C.
1883	Tried farming on the reservation for the first time.
1884	All Crow children were forced to start attending school.
1887	All the Crow Indians were forced to live on reservations, and the old way of life ended.
1904	Became the chief of all the Crow Indians.
1921	Represented all native Americans at the Tomb of the Unknown Soldier in Washington D.C.
1932	Died.

Student 2: Complete the questions below by putting one word in each blank. Ask your partner the questions and write down the answers.

Example:

When _____was_____ Daly born?   Answer: _____1848_____

1. When _____ he emigrate to _____ United States?
2. When _____ he sent to Montana by his company?
3. What _____ he do in 1880?
4. What _____ he plan in 1883?
5. When _____ he become a millionaire?
6. What happened _____ 1888?
7. What company _____ the world's largest producer _____ copper _____ 1895?
8. When _____ Daly die?

Activity 19   *Use It!*

Look at the answers to the questions you asked each other in Activity 18. Write at least five sentences about events in the lives of Daly and Plenty Coups. Use a different word group from the list below in each sentence.

Example:

By the time. . . , . . . had
By the time Plenty Coups became the chief of all the Crow, Anaconda had become a city.

was. . . years old when	By the time. . . , . . . had
had already . . . when	dead for . . . years when
had been . . . for. . . years when	about the same time that
had not yet . . . when	three years before
Before. . . , . . . had	one year after

Activity 20   *Use It!*

Make a table of important dates in your own life like the tables in Activity 18. Work with a partner. Make sentences about both your lives similar to those in Activity 19.

 **Lesson Four**

The Before-Future Tenses

Point to Remember: The Before-Future Tense ••••••••••••••••••••••••••••••••••

We use the **before-future tense** to indicate that an action in the future will end before another action or before a specific time in the future.

Active example:

By the time the polls close tonight, hundreds of thousands of Montanans **will have** cast[3] their votes.[1]

Passive example:

By the time the polls close tonight, hundreds of thousands of votes **will have been**[1] [3] cast[3] in Montana.

Activity 21   *Practice It!*

Put each verb in the correct tense. Use only the before-past, before-present, or before-future tenses. Use the passive voice where necessary.

Example:

A week ago, Betty's car was brand new. Nobody (ever/drive) had ever driven it. She (drive) has driven it about two hundred miles up to now. She thinks that by this time next year, she (drive) will have driven it almost 8,000 miles.

1. A week ago, Betty's car was brand new. It (never/drive) _____
    _____. As of this moment, it (drive) _____ about two hundred
    miles. By this time next year, it (probably[1]/drive) _____
    more than 8,000 miles.

2. The XYZ Widget Company is doing very well. By June 30 of last year, the company
    (sell) _____ 750,000 widgets in 62 different countries. So far this year
    (June 30), the company (sell) _____ over 900,000 widgets in 72 countries.
    The company's board of directors is sure that by June 30 of next year, the XYZ Widget
    Company (sell) _____ over 1,000,000 widgets in over 80 countries.

---

[1]Put the adverb *probably* before or after the power word.

3. Justin's playing golf. Right now, he's at the fourth tee. He (just/tee) _____ _____ off, and he is watching the ball sail into the air. So far, he (have) _____ a good game. He (hit) _____ the ball eleven times, which is just one over par.

4. One country has a poor record in saving its rain forest. By 1950, only 3% of the rain forest (cut) _____ down. As of today, more than 40% (cut) _____ down. At the present rate of destruction, all the country's rain forest (cut) _____ down by the year 2023.

Activity 22   *Use It!*

Write five predictions about your own future. (**Note:** If you don't feel confident about your predictions, you may want to write structures like: *I will probably have* + Form 3, and *I hope to have* + Form 3.)

Example of a prediction made by Patty:

"By the time I finish my first term as governor, I will have brought one thousand new jobs to Montana."

Points to Remember: The Progressive Before-Future Tense · · · · · · · · · · · · · · · ·

❶ We use the **progressive before-future tense** to indicate that an action will begin and continue until a specific time in the future.

Active example:

By the time the polls close tonight, people **will have been voting** for fifteen hours.

❷ This tense is rarely used in the passive voice.

Activity 23   *Practice It!*

Look at Bobby Newton's schedule on page 82. Your teacher will give you a specific time of day. What will Bobby already have done by that time next Tuesday? Study the schedule for 30 seconds. Then close the book, and say as many of his activities as you can remember.

Examples:

Teacher: 1:15 P.M.

By 1:15 P.M. next Tuesday, Bobby will already have had breakfast.
By 1:15 P.M. next Tuesday, Bobby will have been practicing Tai Chi for 45 minutes.

Activity 24   *Practice It!*

Choose the best verb for each blank, and put it in the correct form. Use active and passive voices. Put power words in the boxes.

Example:

Betty (have, make) _____had_____ a great time in Las Vegas.

1. It's 2:30 P.M. Right now, Betty (sit, stand) _____ in her favorite chair. She (think, sit) _____ down 20 minutes ago. That means that she (sit, work) _____ for 20 minutes. If she (finish, stay) _____ there until 2:50, she (stay, sit) _____ there for a total of 50 minutes.

2. At the time of Jesus, there (have, be) _____ about 250,000,000 people in the world. By 1750, the world's population (reach, fall) _____ only 725,000,000. At about that time, however, world population (stop, start) _____ to grow rapidly. By 1990, the population (decrease, increase) _____ to 5,333,000,000 people. Social scientists predict that the world's population (grow, shrink) _____ to 12 billion by the end of the 21st century if nothing (do, fall)[1] _____ to discourage people from (have, be) _____ so many children. The question that (enjoy, concern) _____ social scientists the most is this: ☐ the Earth (be, seem) _____ able to support 12 billion people comfortably? Many (believe, check) _____ that it ☐ not.

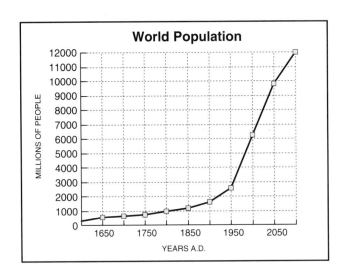

3. By the time the election workers (finish, start)[2] _____ counting votes around 9:00 A.M. tomorrow, they (count, vote) _____ for twelve hours straight.

---

[1] Use simple present tense in *if* clauses about the future.

[2] Use simple present tense in future time clauses with *by the time, when, after, before*, etc.

Activity 25   *Practice It!*

Choose the best verb for each blank, and put it in any correct tense. Put power words in the boxes.

Examples:

Today Patty (go/get) _____got_____ up early, but tomorrow, she (stay, walk) _is going to stay_ in bed until noon.

1. Today is Sammy's eighteenth birthday. Right now, he's standing in the doorway of an airplane high over the rolling farmland of Eastern Montana. He (watch, listen) _____ his older sister Clare, who [_____] just (run, jump) _____ out of the plane. Clare (swim/parachute) _____ for eight years, but this will be Sammy's first jump. Until today, his parents (allow, forbid) _____ him to skydive.

Sammy

Clare

Now

2. Sammy's ready! He (put on, take off) _____ his parachute. Of course, he (have, be) _____ nervous. Who wouldn't be? As soon as the instructor (whisper, yell) _____ "go," he (fly, skydive) _____ for the first time in his life! One thing is sure: He (forget, remember) _____ this jump as long as he (die, live) _____.

3. On the ground, Clare has run over to meet Sammy after his first jump.

C: How (be, take) _____ it, Sammy?

S: Fantastic! [_____] you (work, see) _____ me?

C: I sure [_____]. My little brother! A sky–diver! [_____] you really (excite, enjoy) _____ it?

S: Yeah! I' [_____] never (do, make) _____ anything so exciting in my whole life! I (think, want) _____ to jump again!

C: Today? Now? I [_____] not usually (do, jump) _____ more than once in a day, but…

S: Come on, Clare! It's my birthday today! I _____ (wait, expect) for this day for eighteen years! Come on! Jump with me!

C: OK! Let's go! We have to hurry. The plane (turn on, take off) _____ in about 20 minutes. We have to go to the clubhouse to get two more parachutes. Remember, the parachutes have to (carefully/listen, carefully/check) _____ before we can jump.

S: And I (have, think) _____ to go to the car to get some more money.

C: Forget it, Sammy. I (need, want) _____ this to be my birthday gift to you!

S: Wow! Thanks!

Activity 26   *Use It!*

Write a dialogue similar to the one in Activity 25, between two people who have just had a great adventure of some kind. When you finish, underline all examples of before-focus tenses. Here are some possible adventures:

1. a visit to a big city
2. a first camping trip
3. participation in a sporting event
4. a musical event
5. a theatrical event
6. an encounter with a large animal
7. a hunting or fishing trip
8. water skiing

Chapter 8

THE AFTER-FOCUS TENSES

 Lesson 1

The After-Present Tenses

Points to Remember: The Simple After-Present Tenses ·······················

❶ The **simple after-present tenses** are the same as the future tenses.

Active example:

a. If Patty wins, she $\left\{\begin{array}{l}\textbf{is going to}\\ \textbf{will}\end{array}\right\}$ **stop** the construction of the dam.

Passive example:

b. If Patty loses, the dam $\left\{\begin{array}{l}\textbf{is going to}\\ \textbf{will}\end{array}\right\}$ **be built**.

❷ *Will* and *be going to* can both be used in making **predictions** about the future.

A campaign worker said, "I feel sure Patty $\left\{\begin{array}{l}\textbf{is going to}\\ \textbf{will}\end{array}\right\}$ win the election!"

❸ *Going to* is used more than *will* to express **plans** for the future. Patty can express her plans with *going to* or *planning to*:

Interviewer: Well, Ms. Flick, the campaign is almost over. Tell me, do you have any plans for relaxation after the election.

Patty: I'm $\left\{\begin{array}{l}\textbf{going to}\\ \textbf{planning to}\end{array}\right\}$ take a camping trip next week.

The same sentence with *will* would not be a good answer to the interviewer's question.

❹ If you are unsure whether to use *will* or *be going to*, choose *be going to*. It is almost always correct.

Activity 1   *Study It!*

Patty and Betty have a cousin named Shirly. Shirly has just gotten engaged to Dale, a young man she met a week ago.

Facts About Dale

Age:	20
From:	Otter, Montana (a small town)
Major:	agriculture
Hobbies:	hunting, skiing, video games

Facts About Shirly

Age:	19
From:	San Francisco
Major:	business
Hobbies:	classical music, museums, dancing

Dale and Shirly are both very excited about their engagement. Both are on the phone talking to their best friends. Dale is talking with Bill, and Shirly is talking with Donna. Bill and Donna ask the same questions about their friends' plans.

Donna and Bill's Questions

1. When's the wedding going to be?
2. What kind of wedding are you going to have?
3. What are you going to do about your educations?
4. Are you both going to work outside the home? (Explain your answer.)
5. How many kids are you going to have?
6. When are you going to have the first kid?
7. Who's going to take care of the kids when they're young?
8. What kind of town are you going to live in?
9. Where are you going to live?
10. Where are you going to go for vacations?

Dale   Bill   Donna   Shirly

Activity 2   *Use It!*

Step 1:   Divide the class into groups of men and women. If this is not possible, divide in any convenient way. Each group should have from two to four people.

Step 2:   Men's groups will write Dale's answers to Bill's questions. Women's groups will write Shirly's answers to Donna's questions. Because you are talking about plans, you should use *be going to* in every answer.

> **Example:**
>
> *Question:*   How far are you going to live from your parents?
> *Answer:*   We're going to live in the same town as my parents.

Step 3:   Compare the men's answers with the women's answers.

Step 4:   Make some predictions about Shirly and Dale's future. For predictions, you can use *will* or *going to*.

> **Example:**
>
> I think they $\left\{ {are\ going\ to \atop will} \right\}$ live in a small town near a big city.

Points to Remember: The Progressive After-Present Tenses ·····················

❶ The progressive after-present tenses, which are the same as the progressive future tenses, can be used to express an action that will be in progress at a specific future time.

> With luck, Patty $\left\{ {\textbf{is going to} \atop \textbf{will}} \right\}$ **be celebrating** at 11:30 tonight.

❷ Often, there is not much difference between the progressive after-present tenses and the simple after-present tenses.

> If Patty loses the election, UEC $\left\{ {\textbf{is going to} \atop \textbf{will}} \right\}$ $\left\{ {\textbf{build} \atop \textbf{be building}} \right\}$ the dam.

❸ These tenses are not often used in the passive voice.

Activity 3   *Practice It!*

Look at Bobby Newton's schedule on page 82. For each time your teacher gives, say what Bobby will be doing next Tuesday.

> **Example:**
>
> 12:30 P.M.
>
> Bobby $\left\{ {is\ going\ to \atop will} \right\}$ be practicing Tai Chi at 12:30 P.M. next Tuesday.

Activity 4   *Use It!*

What will you and your classmates be doing in the year 2020? Interview a classmate and write at least five sentences about what he/she will be doing in that year. Include jobs, home life, hobbies, sports, etc. Use the simple and progressive after-present tenses.

Example:

In the year 2020, Frankie will be living in Jakarta.

If your classmate is not sure about his/her future, you may want to begin your sentence like this:

Frankie hopes to be working. . .
Frankie will probably be living. . .

 **Lesson 2**

The After-Past Tenses

Points to Remember ···

❶ In the active voice, there is often not much difference between the **progressive** and **simple after-past tenses.**

When Betty started gambling at 8:32 P.M., she knew that she $\left\{ \begin{array}{l} \textbf{was going to} \\ \textbf{would} \end{array} \right\}$ $\left\{ \begin{array}{l} \textbf{lose} \\ \textbf{be losing} \end{array} \right\}$ tens of thousands of dollars.

❷ A verb expressing an action in progress at a specific time after the past focus should be in the progressive tense.

When Bobby Newton got up last Tuesday at 11:00 A.M., he knew he $\left\{ \begin{array}{l} \textbf{was going to} \\ \textbf{would} \end{array} \right\}$ **be driving** to work at 3:45 P.M.

❸ Generally, only the simple after-past tense is used in the passive voice.

When Justin sent Betty to Las Vegas, he hoped that her picture $\left\{ \begin{array}{l} \textbf{was going to} \\ \textbf{would} \end{array} \right\}$ **be published** in *The Capital Times.*

Activity 5   *Practice It!*

Look at Bobby Newton's schedule on page 82. Since Bobby's activities are exactly the same every working day, he knew when he got up last Tuesday what he would be doing at different times during the day. For each time your teacher gives, say what Bobby knew he would be doing.

Example:

12:15 P.M.
When Bobby got up last Tuesday, he knew that he would be taking a shower at 12:15 P.M.

Activity 6   *Practice It!*

Choose the best verb for each blank, and put it in the correct tense. Use active and passive voices. Put power words in the boxes.

Example:

✔ expect   ✔ know

When Betty agreed to go to Las Vegas, she [did] *not* ____know____ *how much money she* ____would be expected____ *to lose.*

Group 1

buy   build   bury

1. Alexia said she _____ a camera when she went out on Saturday morning. But when she came back, she was driving a new car that she [   ] just _____.

2. When the Pharaoh Khufu _____ his pyramid, he knew his body _____ in it after he died.

Group 2

want   come   return   win   tell

3. (*A reporter is interviewing Wendy Smith, who has just become Miss America.*)

   R: Congratulations, Wendy, on becoming the new Miss America. Tell me: When you _____ to Dallas eight days ago, did you think that you _____?

   W: No, I really [   ] not. The other girls are so beautiful and so talented. When I heard Miss Arizona play the piano, I _____ myself that there was no way for me to win.

   R: What [   ] you plan to do after your year as Miss America?

   W: I _____ to my job in the hospital. I _____ to continue helping patients. I think that's the most important thing I can do.

   R: It certainly [   ], Wendy. Well, congratulations again!

Group 3

make   make   like   have   smell

4. R: I hope you _____ moussaka, Jill.

    J: I [   ] never _____ moussaka, Roger, but I always
         like to try new foods. It _____ delicious!

    R: It's an old family recipe. Why, I _____ moussaka as long as I
         can remember.

    J: What's in it?

    R: Ground lamb and egg plant underneath. The topping _____
         of milk, egg, and flour.

    J: Sounds great to me.

Activity 7   *Use It!*

Step 1:   Certainly your plans for the future have changed since you were younger–say, one half of
              your present age. Write one sentence saying what you used to think you were going to be
              or do later in life and what you think you are going to be or do now.

       Example:

       *When I was nine, I thought I was going to become a fire fighter, but now I think I am going to
       be a movie star.*

Step 2:   Read your sentence out loud. A classmate will repeat your sentence.

       Example:

       Student 1:   *When I was nine, I thought I was going to become a fire fighter, but now I think
                      I'm going to be a movie star.*

       Student 2:   *When Lisa was nine, she thought she was going to become a fire fighter, but now
                      she thinks she is going to be a movie star.*

Chapter 9

ALL TENSES

Activity 1   *Read It!*

The composition below is a **word photograph** or **word photo.** It describes the "photo" below. Like a photo, the composition is a "picture" of a specific place at a specific point in time. Read it.

     This is a picture of a family camping on a river in Montana right now. In the foreground, 16-year-old Pete has just cast his line into the river. He's been fishing for only half an hour, and he's already caught two fish. He's hoping to get another.

     Farther down the river, his mother hasn't been having such good luck. Her fishing line has just snapped, and the fish, a real beauty, is going to get away. She's lost three fish so far today, and she's very upset. The fish, on the other hand, is quite happy to be free again, but he's not enjoying having a hook in his mouth. This is the second time he's been caught and gotten away, so he has plenty of stories to tell his fish friends.

     The family is planning to have fish for breakfast. Pete's dad is sitting by the camp stove cooking one of the fish that Pete has caught. He's using a stove because building a fire harms the environment. Pete's dad is a pretty good cook.

     Pete's 5-year-old brother, Sam, is still sleeping. He's been sleeping for 11 hours. He's going to wake up soon, but he's not going to get up until breakfast is ready. In the background, a hungry raccoon is looking into the campsite. He's hoping to get a piece of fish for breakfast, too.

Activity 2   *Analyze It!*

Step 1:   Discuss these questions.
           What is the time focus of the composition?
           Does the focus change at any point?

Step 2: Find two examples of each of the following structures in the word photo on page 99. Underline them and label them with the letter of the structure.

   a. simple present
   b. progressive present
   c. after-present with *going to*
   e. before-present
   f. progressive before-present
   g. plans and hopes

Examples:

       a
"This is a picture of a family camping on a river in Montana right now.

                                 e
In the foreground, 16-year-old Pete has just cast his line into the river."

Activity 3   *Use It!*

Step 1: Draw (or find) a picture with at least three people in it. For best results, make or choose a picture with a lot of activity.

Step 2: Write a description of the picture. Include at least two examples of each tense listed in Step 2 of Activity 2, and label them as you did there. The focus is right now, so use only those present focus tenses. Like a photograph, your description can have only one focus: right now. (**Note:** Do not include expressions like *then, after that,* and *next.* These expressions indicate a change of focus, and the focus never changes in a photo or in a word photo.)

Activity 4   *Practice It!*

Imagine that you are a member of Pete's family. You are telling a friend about the picture, which was taken during your fishing trip to Montana three years ago. Complete the new word photo. (**Note:** Notice the verb tenses in the example below. When you tell somebody about a snapshot, you can use present tense in sentences like "That's me there." and "I don't remember," but most of your description should be in the past focus tenses.)

Example:

This is a picture of our fishing trip to Montana three years ago. That's me there. I'd just cast my line. I'd already caught seven or eight fish even though I'd only been fishing for a little while. I guess I was hoping to catch another. I don't remember how many fish I caught that day.

Activity 5   *Use It!*

Imagine that you are one of the people in your own word photo and that the photo was taken a long time ago. You are now telling a friend about it using the past focus tenses.

Chapter 10

VERBS FOLLOWED BY GERUNDS AND INFINITIVES

 Lesson 1

A Look at Infinitives and Gerunds after Verbs

Activity 1   *Read It!*

Step 1: In "The Big River Mix-Up," two-year-old Patty is saved by a wolf. Can wolves really take care of human children? Maybe they can. According to Reverend J. A. L. Singh, a missionary in India, two "wolf-children" were found in 1920.[1] Read the story.

Reverend Singh and his wife ran an orphanage.[2] In September of 1920, some people from a nearby village led him to a place where they claimed to have been frightened by ghosts.

Singh found an enormous ant-hill[3] with tunnels going into it. He watched as three full-grown wolves came out of the mound, followed by two cubs.[4] Then came two terrible looking creatures with human bodies, but with so much filthy hair that their heads looked enormous. Singh realized that these "ghosts" were human children.

Singh hired some men to dig the creatures out the next day. The three adult wolves again came out. The first two ran away, but the third, a she-wolf, threatened to attack the men. Singh had told the men not to shoot, but some of them killed the she-wolf anyway.

The men opened up the ant mound and found the two cubs and the two children. They were girls. They were holding on to each other in one big ball. They growled[5] and showed their teeth as they were wrapped up in sheets, with only their heads sticking out. They did not seem to appreciate being captured in that way.

Vocabulary

[1] J. A. L. Singh and Robert M. Zingg, *Wolf Children and Feral Man* (Archon Books, 1966)
[2] an orphanage: a home for children without parents
[3] an ant-hill: a hill of earth in which ants, a kind of insect, live
[4] a cub: a young wolf
[5] to growl: to make a warning noise, like a dog

Singh took them to the orphanage. The younger girl, whom the Singhs called Amala, appeared to be about one and a half. The older, whom the Singhs called Kamala, looked about eight. It was surprising that the girls resembled wolves in some ways. Their teeth were more pointed than normal human teeth, and their eyes glowed in the dark. Unable to walk upright, they could move very quickly on all fours.

The girls did not enjoy being with other children. They avoided being touched. They refused to wear normal clothing. They didn't like eating normal food; they preferred to have raw meat and sometimes caught birds.

Amala died after about a year in the orphanage. Kamala lived until 1929. By that time, the Singhs had taught her to walk upright. She had accepted wearing clothes, had learned to speak very simply, and had begun to prefer cooked meat to raw. She had also grown in trust and love for the missionary couple and some of the other children.

Is Singh's story true? Nobody will ever know. In the 1970s, a British writer named Charles Maclean went to India to investigate—a difficult task after more than 40 years. In the end, however, Maclean decided that Singh's story was basically true, but that he had probably made up some parts of it. If Maclean is right, the reverend's reasons for not telling the whole truth remain a mystery.[1]

Step 2: Discuss these questions: What do you think? Can Singh's story be true?

Step 3: This story has a number of verbs followed by **gerunds** or **infinitives.** Some examples are given below. How many more examples of these structures can you find?

   a. The girls did not **enjoy being** with other children.
   b. Amala **appeared to be** about one and a half.
   c. Reverend Singh **hired** some men **to dig** the girls out.

Points to Remember: Gerunds and Infinitives After Verbs ....

❶ In these structures, the first verb has tense. The second verb has form, but no tense.

   a. When Patty was a little girl, she **enjoyed playing** with all kinds of animals, especially dogs.
                                       gerund

   b. The men **had been trying to open** the ant-hill for only a few seconds when the three adult wolves came out. infinitive

❷ In some cases, the two verbs share the same subject.

                  V1   V2
   Reverend Singh **hoped to teach** the wolf-children his religion.

   Reverend Singh is the subject of Verb 1 and of Verb 2.

❸ In other cases, however, the two verbs have different subjects.
        S1   V1   S2   V2
   Reverend Sing, wanted Kamala to walk like a normal child.

---

[1] Charles Macleon, *The Wolf Children* (New York: Hill & Wang, 1977) p. 301-302.

 **Lesson 2**

Verbs Followed by Infinitives

Point to Remember: Verbs Followed by Infinitives ··························

The verbs in the table below can be followed directly by an infinitive. That means that there is only one subject in the structure. Verbs with related meanings are grouped together. Verbs with asterisks (*) can also be followed by gerunds.

Verbs Followed by Infinitives: One Subject Only

Verbs	Examples
agree, accept, consent	Betty agreed (accepted, consented) to go to Las Vegas.
appear, seem	Amala and Kamala did not appear (seem) to be completely human.
attempt, try	Justin has been attempting (trying) to hurt Patty's chances for success.
ask, beg	After his first visit to Wall Street, Justin asked (begged) to go back.
begin,* start*	Soon after Ruth and Leroy Flick took her to their home, she began (started) to talk to an imaginary friend she called Betty.
claim	Both Patty and Hal Miller claim to be the best candidate.
continue*	Ruth and Leroy Flick were good parents to little Patty, but she continued to cry a lot for several months.
demand	The angry ranchers demanded to talk to the governor about bear attacks on their cattle.
fail	Reverend Singh failed to protect the she-wolf.
forget	Today is election day! Don't forget to vote!
hate,* can't stand*	To this day, she hates (can't stand) to travel in airplanes.
have to, need	In some counties, all adults have (need) to vote. It's the law.
learn	Betty learned to play roulette before going to Las Vegas.
like,* love*	Little Patty liked (loved) to play with dogs.
mean, plan, intend	Patty means (plans, intends) to stop the construction of the dam if elected.
prefer*	Of all ways to relax, Patty prefers to go camping alone.
pretend	Betty pretended to be a rich woman who didn't care about losing thousands.
promise	Justin promised to pay Betty $150,000 when she returned from Las Vegas.
refuse	At first, Kamala and Amala refused to let anyone touch them.
remember	As a candidate, Patty must remember to comb her hair and put on fresh make up before every public appearance.
say	"Justin said to enjoy myself!"[1] Betty thought as she bet another $7,000.
threaten	By the early 1800's, the arrival of thousands of whites in Montana was threatening to destroy the Indians' way of life.
want, hope, would like	Patty wants (hopes, would like) to make many changes in the government.

---

[1] This means: "Justin told me to enjoy myself."

103

Activity 2   *Practice It!*

Choose the best verb for each blank, and put it in the correct form.

Example:

✔ want   ✔ discredit

Justin sent Betty to Las Vegas because he ___wanted___ *to* ___discredit___ *Patty.*

Group 1

    fail   get   be   pretend

1. If you _____ to _____ a visa, there is no way for you to enter that country.

2. The little girl _____ to _____ Buffalo Woman yesterday.

Group 2

    rain   threaten   study   remember

3. _____ to _____ for tomorrow's test!

4. Look at those black clouds! It _____ to _____. We'd better bring the laundry in from the back yard!

Group 3

    demand   promise   give   tease   refuse   see

5. In the restaurant last night, an angry customer _____ to _____ the manager.

6. The student was upset because the teacher _____ to _____ him a make-up test last week.

7. After being scolded, the little boy always _____ not to _____ his little sister anymore.

Group 4

    hunt   hand in   consent   let   learn   forget

8. Kuni was very angry with himself because he _____ to _____ his assignment to the teacher.

9. Reverend Singh didn't always _____ to _____ visitors see the wolf-children.

10. Young Crow boys _____ to _____ buffalo in the old days.

Activity 3   *Use It!*

Step 1: Imagine an interview with a famous or interesting person of the past. Write down the name of the person, a short description, the date of the interview, and the person's approximate age at that time.

Examples:

Reverend J. A. L. Singh: an Indian missionary who claimed to have found two young girls living with wolves.
Interview date: 1931. Approximate age at that time: 53.

Step 2: Using your knowledge and imagination, complete ten of the following sentences as your interviewee might have done.

Example:

When I was very young, I learned to…
When I was very young, I learned to appreciate wild animals.

As a child, I used to pretend to. . .

Once, _____ begged me to. . .

Once, _____ threatened to _____, but I. . .

Once, I promised to. . .

In my kind of work, one must never forget to. . .

Every day, I have to. . .

I hate to. . .

I have always refused to. . .

I have never consented to. . .

When I was _____ years old, I started to. . .

I regret that I failed to. . .

I intend to. . .

I love to. . .

Someday, I would like to. . .

 **Lesson 3**

Verbs Followed by a Second Subject and an Infinitive

Point to Remember: Verbs Followed by a Second Subject and an Infinitive · · · ·

The verbs in the table below can be followed by a second subject and an infinitive. Verbs with related meanings are grouped together.

Verbs Followed by a Second Subject and an Infinitive

Verbs	Examples
advise, encourage, urge	Patty's campaign manager advised (encouraged, urged) her to explain everything on TV.
allow, permit	Reverend Singh did not allow (permit) Amala and Kamala to leave the orphanage alone.
ask, beg, implore	The woman asked (begged, implored) the President to increase the budget for medical research.
cause, require, force	The law caused (required, forced) the mining company to rebuild the land after removing the coal.
convince, persuade, get	Will Patty be able to convince (persuade, get) Montanans to vote for her?
expect	In spite of the gambling incident, many folks expect Patty to win.
forbid	The Singhs forbade the other children to tease Kamala.
help[1]	The manager's job is to help Patty to run her campaign.
hire	Patty hired her manager to run her campaign for her.
invite	Justin invited Betty go to dinner with him.
need	Every campaign needs volunteers to go door-to-door giving out political information.
remind	Patty's manager always reminds her to smile more on TV.
teach	The Singhs taught Kamala to walk upright.
tell, order command	Justin told (ordered, commanded) his assistant not to talk with, anybody about Betty's trip to Las Vegas.
want, would like	Many people want (would like) Patty to win the election.
warn	After the Las Vegas incident, Patty's campaign manager warned Patty to tell him where she would be every minute of every day.

---

[1] The word *to* can be omitted after *help*: Correct: *The manager's job is to help Patty run her campaign.*

Activity 4   *Practice It!*

Step 1: Read each mini-dialogue and choose the best verb.

Step 2: Write a sentence summarizing the situation. Be sure to put the main verb in the correct tense according to the time indicator.

Example:

last week

Best verb: ☐ convince   ☐ need   ☑ urge

The doctor ___urged the patient to get more exercise___.

1. a couple of months ago

    Justin: Hi, Betty. You know, there's a nice new seafood restaurant on Daly Avenue. Would you like to have dinner there with me next Saturday?

    Betty: Why, yes… . Er, of course… . That would be very nice… Ah, what time?

    Best verb: ☐ remind   ☐ invite   ☐ forbid

    Justin _____

2. yesterday

    Mother: You'd better not climb that little tree. It looks shaky to me.
    Child: Awwww, Mom! It'll be okay.

    Best verb: ☐ remind   ☐ warn   ☐ forbid

    The woman _____

3. tomorrow

    Mother: You may not climb that tree.
    Child: Awwww, Mom! It'll be okay.
    Mother: Absolutely not!

    Best verb: ☐ warn   ☐ beg   ☐ forbid

    The woman_____

4. last year

    Father: You may go to the amusement park next Saturday.
    Child: Really? Gee, thanks Dad.

    Best verb: ☐ convince   ☐ allow   ☐ expect

    The man _____

5. a couple of months ago

   Justin: Oh, there's just one other little thing I forgot to mention.
   Betty: Oh?
   Justin: Well, we'd like to pay for you to visit the best hairdresser in Las Vegas.
   Betty: You want to change my appearance?
   Justin: We just want you to have your hair a certain way, that's all.
   Betty: I'm not so sure, Justin. This sounds…
   Justin: Betty, trust me! You'll be beautiful. And don't forget that the company wants to pay you for your services.
   Betty: I guess maybe I'd prefer not to know everything. Well, okay, Justin.

   Best verb: ☐ persuade   ☐ command   ☐ advise

   Justin _____

6. now

   Instructor: The composition must be typed or word-processed.
   Student: What if I write it in my best handwriting?
   Instructor: No, that will not be acceptable for this assignment.

   Best verb: ☐ encourage   ☐ get   ☐ expect

   The instructor_____

7. 1835

   Commander: Soldier, take this note to the general.
   Soldier: Yes, sir!

   Best verb: ☐ order   ☐ invite   ☐ warn

   The commander _____

8. twelve years ago

   Patty: Of course, Governor, we want to improve the economy of Montana. But building coal-fired generating plants is not the best solution.
   Governor: Why not?
   Patty: We have clean air and clean water. Burning coal is a dirty way to produce electricity. Also, if we build 21 new generating plants here, there'll be high-voltage transmission lines everywhere, destroying our beautiful vistas. Governor, please! Montana won't be Montana anymore if we build these plants.

   Best verb: ☐ beg   ☐ help   ☐ convince

   Patty _____

Activity 5   *Use It!*

Work in groups of three or four. In each item, write a general statement about the two groups of people. Use *should* and one of the verbs given. (**Note:** All the students in your group must agree that the sentence is both true and correct.)

Examples:

teachers (help, warn, hire) students
Teachers should help their students to understand the lessons.

1. citizens (warn, help, tell) politicians
2. husbands (forbid, allow, encourage) wives
3. wives (urge, forbid, tell) husbands
4. government (forbid, force, help) people
5. fathers (force, urge, teach) sons
6. mothers (persuade, require, teach) daughters
7. adult children (ask, force, encourage) elderly parents
8. journalists (remind, help, forbid) readers
9. bosses (expect, remind, help) subordinates
10. subordinates (expect, remind, help) bosses

 # Lesson 4

Verbs Followed by Gerunds

Points to Remember: Verbs Followed by Gerunds ·

❶ Many verbs can be followed by gerunds. In the following examples, the two verbs share one subject.

   a. So many visitors wanted to see the wolf-children that the Singhs sometimes **denied keeping** them at the orphanage.

   b. Betty **is considering taking** a trip to Hawaii.

❷ If the two verbs have different subjects, the subject of the gerund is usually in the possessive form in formal language.

   a. In his diary, Reverend Singh mentioned **Kamala's** catching and eating several birds.

   b. Many years later, one of the orphans remembered **Kamala's** biting her.

❸ In the table below, verbs with related meanings are grouped together. Verbs with asterisks (*) can take a second subject.

Verbs Followed by Gerunds

Verbs	Examples
admit	In a conversation with her best friend, Betty admitted having some doubts about the trip to Las Vegas.
appreciate*	Patty appreciates having good campaign workers. Patty appreciates her manager's reminding her to smile on TV.
avoid	Justin avoids talking too much about his work.
can't help, can't resist	Betty can't help (can't resist) buying lots of new clothes.
deny	Justin will deny doing anything wrong if anybody asks him any questions.
enjoy*	Patty doesn't always enjoy having to answer so many questions. She doesn't always enjoy people's asking her so many questions.
finish, complete	Patty finished (completed) writing her speech at 2 A.M.
keep, keep on	Even when very tired, Patty has kept (kept on) campaigning.
look forward to	Patty is looking forward to camping next week. Patty's manager is looking forward to Patty's winning.
mention*	Patty didn't mention going camping to anybody. In a conversation with his boss, Justin didn't mention Betty's going to Las Vegas.
mind*	"I knew you wouldn't mind helping UEC," Justin said to Betty. "Do you mind my smoking?" Justin asked Betty.
miss*	Patty misses being able to travel without being recognized. At first, Betty and Patty missed their mother's singing.
postpone,* put off,* delay*	The manager told Patty not to postpone (put off, delay) explaining everything on TV. The manager did not postpone (put off, delay) Patty's explaining everything.
practice	Justin practices hitting golf balls whenever possible.
quit	Patty will never quit working for the environment.
remember	Patty doesn't remember having a sister.
talk about,* discuss*	Betty talks about (discusses) quitting her job with her best friend. Everybody in Montana was talking about (discussing) Patty's gambling.
think about, consider	Two years ago, a group of citizens asked Patty to think about (consider) running for governor.
tolerate*	If elected, Patty will not tolerate smoking in her office.[1] She will not tolerate other people's smoking

---

[1] In this sentence, the implied subject of the verb *smoking* is *other people*, but it is understood.

Activity 6   Practice It!

Choose the best verb for each each blank, and put it in the correct form.

Example:

✔ get   ✔ appreciate

The police ____appreciate____ ____getting____ information about crimes.

Group 1

   admit   eat   remember   play

1. I'm ashamed to _____ _____ all the chocolates!!

2. When Justin was teaching Betty to play roulette, she said that she didn't
   _____ ever _____ the game before.

Group 2

   put off   change   consider   give

3. The candidate had to _____ _____ his speech because the
   secret service didn't like the venue.

4. Last week, my roommate _____ _____ his major from
   engineering to art history. Finally, he decided to stay in engineering.

Group 3

   finish   appreciate   test   write   talk   miss

5. Some teachers _____ their students' _____ in dark pencil
   or erasable ink.

6. As soon as the engineers _____ _____ the materials, they
   made their recommendation.

7. Betty didn't think she liked Justin very much, so she doesn't really _____
   his _____ to her.

Group 4

   can't help   have   reveal   look forward   deny   stare

8. At tomorrow's hearing, the minister _____ _____ any state
   secrets to the enemy.

9. Most people _____ _____ when they see identical twins.

10. It was very hot on the golf course the other day, and Justin _____ to
    _____ a cold drink after the eighteenth hole.

Activity 7   Use It!

Step 1: The class will work on four different surveys. First, the class counts off by fours. Students
with the number 1 will administer Survey One; students with number 2 will administer
Survey Two, etc.

Step 2: Break into small groups. Each group should have one person with each of the different questionnaires.

Step 3: Ask the other students in your group to close their books. Read each question out loud to the other students in your group and tally the answers: How many say "yes"? How many say "no"? Remember to count yourself.

Step 4: Join with the other students who administered the same questionnaire as you. Tally the complete results with percentages of "yes" and "no" answers.

Step 5: Discuss the results as a class. Write sentences to summarize the results.

Survey One: Attitudes Toward Gambling

Questions	Yes	No
1. Have you ever gambled?	☐	☐
2. Are you against gambling?	☐	☐
3. Do you enjoy taking risks?	☐	☐
4. Do you expect to gamble in the next month?	☐	☐
5. Do you think the government should forbid people to gamble?	☐	☐

Survey Two: Attitudes Toward Business

Questions	Yes	No
1. Do you ever think about going into business?	☐	☐
2. Do you intend to make a lot of money?	☐	☐
3. Are you in favor of having strict laws to control business?	☐	☐
4. Do you mind working very hard?	☐	☐
5. Do you like telling other people what to do?	☐	☐

Survey Three: Attitudes Toward Nature

Questions	Yes	No
1. Do you prefer living in the city to living in the country?	☐	☐
2. Are you interested in camping?	☐	☐
3. Do you enjoy walking in wild places?	☐	☐
4. Would you like to sleep in a tent?	☐	☐
5. If you were a Montanan, would you urge the government to build the dam on the Big River?	☐	☐

Survey Four: Attitudes Toward Political Involvement

Questions	Yes	No
1. Have you ever attended a political demonstration?	☐	☐
2. Do you avoid discussing politics?	☐	☐
3. Do you enjoy giving speeches?	☐	☐
4. If a political party asked you, would you agree to be a candidate in an important election?	☐	☐
5. If you were famous, would you miss being able to travel about freely?	☐	☐

Chapter 11

MODALS AND RELATED STRUCTURES

 Lesson 1

A Look at Modals

Activity 1   *Read It!*

Step 1:   Read the speech.

Folks, I'd like to talk to you about the Big River Valley, the dam, and jobs. Young people have been leaving Montana because jobs here have been disappearing. The people who want the dam say the dam will create jobs. Well, some Montanans might find construction jobs. But once the dam is built, those Montanans will probably find themselves out of work.

You know who wants that dam: a big Chicago energy company! History repeats itself, my friends. We must not forget the strip mines[1] of the 1970s. We should have been paying attention! Those eastern companies took our coal and destroyed our land. A few Montanans may have been made rich, but most of the profits went with the coal—out of state! The dam is the same. The electricity will be sent out, and so will the profits! They'll all go to Chicago!

Folks, we should not have let those Easterners run Montana before! And we should never let them do it again. We should be creating permanent jobs for our young people! High-skill jobs! And the profits must stay in Montana!

You know my position on the environment. It must be protected! The Big River Valley ought to be a good home for bears and mountain lions. And Montana ought to be a good home for people! We don't have to destroy our environment to accomplish that. We could make the Big River Valley a state park and protect it forever. Then we could build an industrial park near the valley for new, clean industries. We can create thousands of good jobs! And we can do it without letting those Easterners make a colony[2] of our state!

Vocabulary

---
[1] a strip mine: a kind of mine at which the land is destroyed to get the coal
[2] a colony: a region controlled by another country, or, in this case, state

Step 2: Discuss these questions.
1. According to Patty, what are Montana's biggest problems?
2. How does she want to solve them?
3. Do you think she's right?

Activity 2   *Analyze It!*

Step 1: Underline the verb phrases with modals in Patty's speech. Discuss their meanings. Is the focus of each expression past, present, future, or the all-time non-focus?

Step 2: Patty uses the six most common modal structures in her speech. Find them and complete the table below. (M) = any modal.

Active Structures	*Examples*
1. (M) + Form 1	*will create, might find*
2. (M) + *be* + Form 5	
3. (M) +	
4. (M) +	

Passive Structures	*Examples*
5. (M) + *be* + Form 3	
6. (M) +	

 # Lesson 2

The Basic Meanings of Modals

Point to Remember: Basic Meanings of Modals ·

The table below explains the basic meanings of some modals.

Meaning	Modal	Example
necessity	must	Candidates **must** campaign if they want to win.
advisability	should/ought to	People $\left\{ \begin{matrix} \textbf{should} \\ \textbf{ought to} \end{matrix} \right\}$ protect the environment.
possibility	may/might	Some Montanans $\left\{ \begin{matrix} \textbf{might} \\ \textbf{may} \end{matrix} \right\}$ benefit from the dam.
capability	can	Patty believes that permanent jobs **can** be created.

Activity 3   *Practice It!*

Choose the best modal and the best verb for each blank.

Example:

✔ should   may   ✔ vote   forget

On election day, people ___should vote___ for the candidates they want to represent them.

Group 1

spend	buy	eat	win
must	can	might	should

1. Betty _____ her money carefully.

2. People _____ in order to live.

3. Nobody knows what will happen. Patty _____ the election.

4. Now that she is rich, Betty _____ some nice things.

Group 2

share	compete	speak	give
must	can	may	should

5. Four-year-old children _____ usually _____ their languages fluently.

6. U.S. workers _____ with workers in many other countries now that industrialization is spreading.

7. Look out! Your teacher _____ you a pop quiz tomorrow!

8. Do you believe that rich people like Justin _____ their money with others?

Group 3

have	accomplish	travel	erupt
must	can	might	should

9. Because Patty refuses to fly, she _____ by car, bus, or train.

10. Some people think that the United Nations _____ more power.

11. The volcano is smoking, and seismologists say that it _____ at any time.

12. Working together, people _____ great things.

Activity 4 Study It!

Next winter, you and two or three of your classmates must spend 30 days in a cabin in the Rocky Mountains of northwest Montana. The average winter temperature there is 26° F (-3° C), and there may be heavy snow. There is no town nearby. Nobody will visit or contact you there. You and your supplies will be transported in and out by helicopter.

The furnished cabin has a living/dining room with a large wood stove, a kitchen, a bathroom, and two sleeping rooms with three beds each. No bedding or appliances are included. Toilet paper is provided. There is cold running water. There is a plug-in water heater between the kitchen and bathroom, but no electric sockets in either room. An enormous pile of uncut fire wood is outside.

A gasoline-powered generator provides just enough electricity for the only two electrical sockets, which are in the living/dining room.

In addition to the clothes he or she is wearing, each person may take one large suitcase containing only clothes, towels, and washcloths, and a smaller case for toiletries. Finally, your group may decide which items to take from the list on page 117.

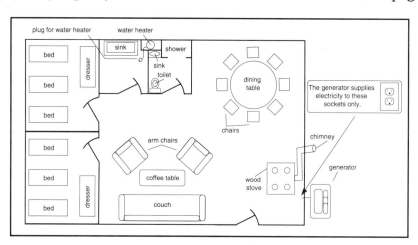

gasoline for the generator

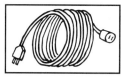

an extension cord with one socket

an ax

an enormous pile of uncut wood

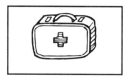

a first aid kit

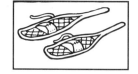

a pair of snowshoes

Activity 5   *Use It!*

Step 1: Work in groups of three or four. Look at the list of items below. Decide as a group how many of each item to take for your 30-day stay in the cabin described in Activity 4. Put the number of each item in the spaces provided. Groups of three cannot take more than 40 items. Groups of four cannot take more than 45 items. (**Note:** You may take any number of any item as long as the total does not exceed the limit for your group. A group of three that began to fill in the table below may have problems later on. Their limit is 40 items, and they have already chosen 21.)

Example:

Items	Number	Items	Number
food for 1 person, 15 days	6	plug-in radios or TVs	2
gasoline to run the generator 25 hours	6	30-foot (9.2 meter) extension cords with only one socket	2
sleeping bag for one person	3	VCRs	1
electric stoves, four burners	1	computers	

Items	Number	Items	Number
food for 1 person, 15 days		plug-in radios or TVs	
gasoline to run the generator 25 hours		30-foot (9.2 meter) extension cords with only one socket	
sleeping bags		VCRs	
electric stoves, four burners		computers	
small electric refrigerators		handguns with 5 bullets each	
one-room electric heaters		musical instruments	
sets of pots and pans		boxes of 5 video cassettes	
boxes of 5 audio cassettes		audio cassette players	
sets of spatulas, large spoons, kitchen knives, etc.		sets of chopsticks, knives, forks, spoons for four people	
sets of dishes, glasses, etc.		sets of fishing equipment	
fire extinguishers		cases of 24 canned beverages	
axes		flashlights with batteries	
show shovels		electric clothes washers	
25-lb (11.8 kg) boxes of books		electric clothes driers	
boxes of pencils, pens, paper		gas lamps	
electric hair driers		100 hours of gas lamp fuel	
first aid kits		pairs of snowshoes	
non-electronic games		sets of cleaning supplies	
plug-in electric lamps		50-foot (15.4 m) clotheslines	

117

Step 2: Write your group's reasons for taking or not taking at least five of the items above. Underline all the modals.

Examples:

We decided to take a pair of snow shoes. It <u>*might*</u> *snow heavily, and snowshoes* <u>*can*</u> *hold us up on deep snow.*
We are not going to take a computer. We <u>*can't*</u> *think of anything to do with one. We* <u>*shouldn't*</u> *waste electricity playing computer games.*

 # Lesson 3

Expressing Necessity

Points to Remember: Present and Future Necessity ························

❶ In affirmative sentences, *have to* has the same meaning as *must*. *Have to* is not a modal because it uses various power words.

Active example:
Young Montanans $\left\{ \begin{array}{l} \textbf{have to} \\ \textbf{must} \end{array} \right\}$ leave the state when they can't find jobs.

Passive example:

A solution $\left\{ \begin{array}{l} \textbf{has to} \\ \textbf{must} \end{array} \right\}$ be found for Montana's problems.

❷ *Have to* can be used in any tense.
   a. Patty **will have to work** hard if elected.
   b. Small animals **have** always **had to protect** themselves from wolves.

❸ *Must* and *have to* have different meanings in negative sentences.
   a. Betty **must not discuss** her trip to Las Vegas with other UEC employees.
       (= Talking is forbidden. If she talks, she might get into serious trouble.)

   b. U.S. citizens **do not have to vote** if they prefer not to.
       (= Voting is not required.)

❹ *Must* has no past form. Only *had to* can be used to express necessity in the past.
       Thirty-seven years ago, the Flicks **had to move** to a new town to avoid questions about their new little girl.

Activity 6   *Practice It!*

In each item, put *must* or *have to* and the verb in parentheses in the correct form. Use affirmative or negative forms and active and passive voices.

Examples:

Little Patty (follow) <u>didn't have to follow</u> the wolf into the woods.
Nobody will ever know why she did it.

Milk (keep) <u>{ must / has to } be kept</u> in a cool place.

1. Customers (smoke) _____ in the no-smoking parts of restaurants.
2. The pilot of an airplane (fall) _____ asleep during a flight.
3. Patty would have preferred to stay in the woods longer, but she (return) _____ to the campaign.
4. Little children (permit) _____ to play in the street.
5. Since she returned from Las Vegas, Betty (be) _____ very careful with money. In fact, she's bought many expensive things.
6. C: (*opens her door*) Hi, Jack! Come on in! We're so glad you could come!
    J: Hi, Carmen. Here. I brought you and Fritz a little something.
    C: Oh, Jack! You (bring) _____ anything.
    J: I know, but I wanted to.
7. Betty was quite upset last Tuesday because the carburetor on her new car (repair) _____.
8. According to state law, the kitchen of the restaurant (thoroughly/clean) _____ at closing time.
9. Spinach (cook) _____. It can be eaten raw like lettuce in salads.
10. I'm sorry I was late for class, Dr. Takada, but I (take) _____ my brother to the airport.

Activity 7   *Use It!*

Step 1: Think of an acquaintance with an unusual or interesting job.
Step 2: Interview a classmate about the advantages and disadvantages of the job he or she has chosen.
Step 3: After an introductory sentence, write four sentences about advantages and four sentences about disadvantages of the job chosen by your classmate. Use *must, must not, doesn't have to* and any other modals you would like.

Examples:

Ong told me about someone he knows who's a bee keeper.
One advantage of being a beekeeper is that one doesn't have to work in an office.
One disadvantage of this job is that a beekeeper may get stung.

 **Lesson 4**

Expressing Advisability

Points to Remember: Present and Future Advisability ·····················

❶ *Should* and *ought to* have the same basic meaning: **advisability**. If something is **advisable**, it is a good idea.

Candidates $\begin{Bmatrix} \text{should} \\ \text{ought to} \end{Bmatrix}$ tell the people the truth.

❷ *Had better* looks like a past tense expression, but it refers to the future.

Justin **had better** keep the Las Vegas mix-up a secret for the rest of his life.

❸ *Had better* is used to express strong advice for a specific occasion. It implies that something bad will happen if the advice is not followed.

Justin **had better** keep the Las Vegas mix-up a secret.
Implication: If he doesn't, he may have to spend time in prison.

Activity 8   *Read It!*

Step 1:   In a recent interview, Patty discussed a possibly serious problem. Read the interview.

Reporter: Frogs disappearing? Is that a problem?

Patty: Let me give you some background. Twenty years ago, I visited a pond in northeastern Montana. It was full of noisy frogs. A month ago, I visited it again, and it was silent. The frogs were gone. This problem has been seen in many areas of the world.

Reporter: Why should we be worried, Ms. Flick?

Patty: Frogs are part of the food chain: frogs eat insects. In turn, larger animals eat frogs. If the frogs disappear, we'll have more insects, and the larger animals will probably starve. It's not just frogs. The whole ecosystem is at risk.

Reporter: What do you suggest?

Patty: If I were governor, I'd instruct the Department of Natural Resources to study this problem. We ought to be working very hard on this.

Reporter: Can the state afford to do that?

Patty: Can the state afford not to? Frogs are disappearing from protected, unpolluted areas, and we have no idea why. Frogs have been on Earth since the age of the dinosaurs. If something is killing them, we'd better find out what it is. Remember, we humans are part of the same ecosystem as frogs.

Step 2: Discuss these questions.

1. What's happening to the world's frogs? Why?
2. Why does Patty consider this a problem?
3. Are you concerned?
4. What solution does Patty suggest?
5. What grammatical structures does she use in her suggestions?

Points to Remember: Past Advisability and Past Mistakes ·

❶ *Should have* + Form 3 and *ought to have* + Form 3 refer to the past.

Active examples:

a. Patty made a mistake. She $\begin{Bmatrix} \text{should} \\ \text{ought to} \end{Bmatrix}$ **have told** somebody about her camping trip.

b. At 10:30 last Tuesday morning, Justin was playing golf. He $\begin{Bmatrix} \text{should} \\ \text{ought to} \end{Bmatrix}$ **have been working.**

Passive example:

c. Patty $\begin{Bmatrix} \text{should not} \\ \text{ought not to} \end{Bmatrix}$ **have been impersonated.**

❷ *Should have* + Form 3 and *ought to have* + Form 3 refer to past mistakes. They refer to things that didn't happen, the opposite of the facts.

d. Patty $\begin{Bmatrix} \text{should} \\ \text{ought to} \end{Bmatrix}$ **have told** somebody. (**Fact:** She didn't tell anybody.)

Activity 9   *Practice It!*

Choose the best verb for each blank and put it in the correct form with *should*, *ought to*, or *had better*. Use *had better* and the progressive when possible. Use active and passive voices. (**Note:** Put a power word in the box in number 4.)

Examples:

✔ go   ✔ rest

Patty ____*should go*____ home and relax today. It's election day!

Sam's friends were surprised to see him at a fraternity party last Friday night. He was very sick. He ____*should have been resting*____ in bed, not out partying.

Group 1

legalize   be   call

1. A: (*knocks on the door*) Room service! Your breakfast is here!

   B: It's about time! It's 9:00. I ordered this meal for 8:30. It _____ _____ here half an hour ago. Now I don't have time to enjoy it.

   A: Sorry, sir. You _____ us at 8:31, as soon as you realized your breakfast was late. We would have brought it immediately.

2. Do you believe that gambling _____ in every country?

Group 2

spank   rest   check

3. Some people believe that children (not) _____ when they misbehave. What about you?

4. A: Look! There's Sam again! He's still sick, and here he is at another party!

   B: He _____ in bed!

   A: He really ⬜ !

5. Before going to Las Vegas, Betty had to pay $15 because she didn't have enough money in her account to cover the check she wrote in the jewelry store. She _____ the balance in her account before writing a check.

Group 3

put   make   eat   go

6. A: Oh my gosh! It's 8:45, and the movie starts at 9:00.

   B: We _____ now, or we'll miss the beginning of the movie.

7. The bed in Betty's hotel room was unmade when she arrived. The bed _____.

8. Justin's nephew Sam helped himself to some ice cream a minute ago. He left the half-full carton on the counter and carried his bowl into the living room. He _____ the carton back in the freezer right now!

9. Sam's mother's rule is "no snacks between meals." Sam (not) _____ _____ right now.

Group 4

watch   hang   stop   vaccinate

10. A: Uh oh! There's only a little gas left in the tank.

    B: Rats! We just passed the last service station for 55 miles. We _____ there to get gas, and I forgot.

    A: No, it's my fault. I _____. After all, I'm the driver.

11. Children _____ against common childhood diseases.

12. Campers in bear country _____ their food from a branch in a tree at least 100 yards from their tent.

Activity 10   *Use It!*

Write an interview of at least 200 words in which a political candidate describes a problem and gives solutions. Underline all modals and expressions of advisability. Use the interview with Patty in Activity 8 as a model.

 **Lesson 5**

Expressing Probability

Activity 11   *Study It!*

Justin is planning to spend this weekend golfing. He was pleased with last Saturday's weather report for the rest of the week: It said that there was a high probability—a good chance—of rain in the beginning of the week, but a low probability of rain near the weekend. The table below gives the chances of rain for each day of the week.

Adverbs Used to Express Probability (Chance)

Day	Chance of Rain	Adverb	Example
Sunday	100%	(none), certainly	It will rain tomorrow. It will **certainly** rain tomorrow.
Monday	95% – 99%	almost certainly	It will **almost certainly** rain on Monday.
Tuesday	65% – 94%	probably	It will **probably** rain on Tuesday.
Wednesday	35% – 64%	maybe, perhaps possibly	(**Maybe/Perhaps**) it will rain on Wednesday. It will **possibly** rain on Wednesday.
Thursday	5% – 34%	probably. . . not	It **probably** will **not** rain on Thursday.
Friday	1% – 4%	almost certainly. . . not	It **almost certainly** will **not** rain on Friday.
Saturday	0%	not, certainly. . . not	It will **not** rain on Saturday. It **certainly** will **not** rain on Saturday

Points to Remember: Using Adverbs to Express Probability ···················

❶ The adverbs *maybe, perhaps, certainly, probably,* and *possibly* can be used in any tense.
   a. The wolf that helped Patty has **almost certainly** died.
   b. **Maybe** Patty saw a wolf on her last camping trip.

❷ The adverbs *maybe* and *perhaps* come at the beginning of a sentence. In affirmative sentences, the adverbs *certainly, probably,* and *possibly* are commonly seen in the following positions:

After the verb *be*:
   a. Justin **is probably** one of the best golfers at UEC.

Before other verbs in the simple present and past:
   b. Patty **certainly works** too hard.

After power words:
   c. Betty **has possibly** decided to quit her job at UEC.

❸ The adverbs *certainly, probably,* and *possibly* commonly come before the power word in negative sentences.
   Patty **certainly will not** go to Las Vegas in the next few years.

Activity 12   *Practice It!*

Add an adverb to each sentence to make it express the probability given in parentheses. Make other necessary changes.

Examples:

Justin enjoys hiking. (20% chance)
Justin probably does not enjoy hiking.

1. It will snow in Miami next August 3rd. (0% chance)
2. Betty expects Justin to call her. (14% chance)
3. It will snow in Chicago next May. (2% chance)
4. Patty will win the election. (52% chance)
5. The extinction of frogs would affect human beings. (97% chance)
6. Betty made reservations for Hawaii yesterday. (81% chance)
7. Advertising encourages children to smoke. (77% chance)
8. Justin sent money to Patty's campaign. (0% chance)
9. Most young people know many popular songs from forty years ago. (6% chance)
10. Betty has enough money to take a world cruise. (87% chance)

Activity 13   *Use It!*

Step 1:   For each probability (0%, 3%, 20%, 49%, 71%, 96%, 100%), write a hunch about a classmate. Write about a different classmate in each sentence. Use an adverb in each sentence. (**Note:** Leave a space after each sentence.)

Examples:

a.   *0% — Ahmad has certainly never eaten raw fish.*
b.   *96% — Keiko almost certainly knows how to arrange flowers.*

Step 2:   Go to each student you wrote about. Change each sentence to a question to check your hunch. (You do not have to write these questions.)

Examples:

a.   *Ahmad, have you ever eaten raw fish?*
b.   *Keiko, do you know how to arrange flowers?*

Step 3:   In the space between your sentences, write an evaluation of your hunch. Your evaluation should be from two to four sentences long.

Examples:

a.   *0% — Ahmad has certainly never eaten raw fish.*
My hunch about Ahmad was wrong. Ahmad's brother once dared him to eat a live goldfish, and he did it.

b.   *96% — Keiko almost certainly knows how to arrange flowers.*
My hunch about Keiko was right. She studied flower arrangement for six years. Flower arrangement is an important art in Japan.

Activity 14   *Read It!*

Step 1:   Modals can be used to express past and present probability. Detective Kim was discussing the Las Vegas incident with two colleagues, Detectives Lopez and Sanders. Read part of their conversation.

Lopez: Why would that woman want to impersonate Patty Flick?

Kim: She **must have wanted** to make Patty lose the election.

Sanders: Somebody [1] **probably** paid her to go to Las Vegas. She [2] **must have been trying** to lose the money!

Kim: Well, who wants Patty to lose? Wait… What's the name of that big company that wants to build the dam on the Big River? They [3] **may have had** something to do with it.

Lopez: They [4.]**can't have given** her all that money. She [5.]**must have lost** $200,000.

Kim: Two hundred thousand? That's nothing! Big companies like UEC often spend two hundred *million* dollars just on a year's advertising.

Lopez: Hmmm. . . [6.]**Maybe** they were involved.

Step 2: Approximately what probability (5%, 25%, etc.) do you think is indicated by each **boldfaced** expression?

Example:

She **must have wanted** . . . about 65% – 99%

Points to Remember: Modals Used to Express Present and Past Probability ⋯

After reading Activity 14 above, study the examples below.

Probability	Modal	Examples (The examples come from the detectives' complete conversation.)
65 – 99%	must	a. The woman **must have wanted** to make Patty lose. b. UEC **must be making** plans for the dam now.
35 – 64%	may, might	c. UEC $\begin{Bmatrix} \text{may} \\ \text{might} \end{Bmatrix}$ **have had** something to do with it. d. UEC $\begin{Bmatrix} \text{may} \\ \text{might} \end{Bmatrix}$ **be paying** people to spy on Patty's campaign.
10 – 34%	must not	e. The woman **must not have had** any money when she left Las Vegas. f. She's very rich. She **must not understand** the financial problems of normal folks.
0 – 5%	can't	g. They **can't have given** her $200,000. h. UEC **can't expect** Montanans to like their dirty work.

Activity 15   *Study It!*

You can add modals of probability to sentences in an almost mathematical way. After reviewing the common modal structures in Activity 2 on page 114, study these examples of "grammar arithmetic." They are all about Patty's best friend, Jill.

Example of the Progressive Present + a Modal:

a. Jill is fishing now.

    + may   (35% – 65% probability)

    Jill may be fishing now.

Example of the Simple Present + a Modal:

b. Jill enjoys camping.

    + must   (65% – 99% probability)

    Jill must enjoy camping.

Example of the Progressive Past + a Modal:

When Patty called Jill at 9:30 last night, the line was busy.

c. Jill was taking a shower at 9:30 last night.

    + must not   (6% – 34% probability)

    Jill must not have been taking a shower at 9:30 last night.

Example of the Progressive Present + a Modal:

d. Jill told Justin about Patty's camping plans.

    + can't   (0% – 5% probability)

    Jill can't have told Justin about Patty's camping plans.

Activity 16   *Practice It!*

Using "grammar arithmetic," add a modal to each sentence to express the probability in parentheses. Make other necessary changes.

Example:

Jill is relaxing now. (59% probability)
Jill may be relaxing now.

1. Jill agrees with Patty on many issues. (98% probability)
2. Jill agrees with Patty on all issues. (2% probability)

3. Jill worked for Patty's campaign. (80% probability)
4. The dinosaurs died out as a result of a meteorite hitting the Earth. (85% probability)
5. Jill was working for Patty's campaign on the third of last month. (40% probability)
6. Several students got a perfect score on the last test. (45% probability)
7. A wolf is hunting near the Big River right now. (40% probability)
8. The natives of North America had a written language before the arrival of the Europeans. (7% probability)
9. Jill saw the Las Vegas picture before Patty did. (43% probability)
10. Jill was pleased with the picture. (0% probability)

Point to Remember: Expressing Future Probability

Only the modals *may* and *might* can be used to express a degree of probability in the future. Adverbs must be used for other probabilities. (See the chart on page 123.)

Probability	Modal	Example
35 – 65%	$\left\{ \begin{matrix} \text{may} \\ \text{might} \end{matrix} \right\}$ + Form 1	Patty $\left\{ \begin{matrix} \text{may} \\ \text{might} \end{matrix} \right\}$ win the election.
	$\left\{ \begin{matrix} \text{may} \\ \text{might} \end{matrix} \right\}$ + be + Form 5	Patty $\left\{ \begin{matrix} \text{may} \\ \text{might} \end{matrix} \right\}$ be celebrating tonight.

Activity 17   *Practice It!*

Rewrite each sentence. Use *may* or *might* if possible. If not, use an adverb.

Example:

There is a 50-50 chance that Betty will keep working at UEC for a few months.
Betty may keep working at UEC for a few months.

1. There is a 20 percent chance that those forests will be protected by the new law.
2. There is a 76 percent chance Justin will avoid Betty when he sees her.
3. There is a 82 percent chance that people will be driving solar cars in future years.
4. There is a 46 percent chance that detectives will identify Betty.
5. There is a 100 percent chance that the sun will rise tomorrow.

Activity 18   *Use It!*

Write at least one sentence about each situation below. Use modals or adverbs in each sentence.

Group 1: Past Situations

Example:

At 10:24 A.M. on July 7, 43 years ago, five-year-old Justin was crying.
He must have been unhappy about something. or He may have fallen off his bike and hurt himself.

1. Sam got a big test back yesterday, and he seemed very upset.
2. Patty was running the water in her kitchen sink last night at 11:10.
3. Rachel was smiling when she left the Financial Aid office yesterday.

Group 2: Present Situations

Example:

My neighbor has a cast on his arm.
He must have a broken arm.

4. That basketball player has not washed his uniform for weeks.
5. Sookhee's roommate is in the language lab every day from nine to noon.
6. That dog scratches itself constantly.

Group 3: Future Situations

Example:

Patty will have been awake for 39 hours when the polls close at 9:00 tonight.
She will probably be very tired.

7. Justin will be going to a resort on Saturday.
8. Patty's going to go camping next weekend.
9. The world record holder in the women's long jump will be competing in next Saturday's track meet.

Group 4: Mixed Focuses

10. My friend and I will have dinner at a restaurant which is famous for its steaks.
11. All the fans in the stadium are cheering.
12. A woman goes into church at 10:00 every morning and comes out at 11:00.

Activity 19   *Use It!*

Student 1 covers page 131 and looks at the pictures below. Student 2 covers this page and looks at the pictures on page 131. Discuss the pictures. Then make at least ten sentences using structures in this chapter.

Examples:

Jack must have taken something important from UEC.
Jack is probably enjoying himself right now.

Jack, Dec. 19 last year

Jack, Dec. 21 last year

Jack, Dec. 21 next year

Duane, Jack, and Darla,
Dec. 20 last year

Jack, now

Activity 20   *Use It!*

Write a conversation of at least 200 words related to "The Big River Mix-Up." It could be between any two characters in the story, for example, between Betty and Justin. Or it could be between any one character in the story and anybody else. For instance, it could be between Betty and the hairdresser, or between Patty and one of her adoptive parents. Include and underline at least five of the structures that you have studied in this chapter.

IRREGULAR VERBS

 Appendix A

be	was/were	been	cut	cut	cut
bear	bore	born[1]/borne			
beat	beat	beat/beaten	deal	dealt	dealt
become	became	become	dig	dug	dug
begin	began	begun	do	did	done
bend	bent	bent	draw	drew	drawn
bet	bet	bet	dream[2]	dreamt	dreamt
bid	bid	bid	drink	drank	drunk
bind	bound	bound			
bite	bit	bitten	eat	ate	eaten
bleed	bled	bled			
blow	blew	blown	fall	fell	fallen
break	broke	broken	feed	fed	fed
bring	brought	brought	feel	felt	felt
broadcast	broadcast	broadcast	fight	fought	fought
build	built	built	find	found	found
burst	burst	burst	fit	fit	fit
buy	bought	bought	flee	fled	fled
			fly	flew	flown
cast	cast	cast	forbid	forbade	forbidden
catch	caught	caught	forget	forgot	forgotten
choose	chose	chosen	forgive	forgave	forgiven
cling	clung	clung	freeze	froze	frozen
come	came	come			
cost	cost	cost	get	got	got/gotten[3]
creep	crept	crept	give	gave	given

---

[1] Form 3 of *bear* is born in sentences like: I was **born** in New Jersey. It is *borne* in sentences like: They have **borne** this burden for many years.

[2] This verb can also be regular.

[3] In American English, Form 3 of *get* is *gotten* except in expressions like: I've **got** a problem. She's **got** to finish this work.

go	went	gone	pay	paid	paid
grind	ground	ground	prove	proved	proved[6]
grow	grew	grown	put	put	put
hang	hung	hung[4]	quit	quit	quit
have	had	had			
hear	heard	heard	read	read	read
hide	hid	hidden	rid	rid	rid
hit	hit	hit	ride	rode	ridden
hold	held	held	ring	rang	rung
hurt	hurt	hurt	rise	rose	risen
			run	ran	run
keep	kept	kept			
kneel[5]	knelt	knelt	say	said	said
know	knew	known	see	saw	seen
			seek	sought	sought
lay	laid	laid	sell	sold	sold
lead	led	led	set	set	set
leap[5]	leapt	leapt	shake	shook	shaken
leave	left	left	shed	shed	shed
lend	lent	lent	shine	shone	shone[7]
let	let	let	shoot	shot	shot
lie	lay	lain	show	showed	shown
light	lit	lit	shrink	shrank	shrunk[8]
lose	lost	lost	shut	shut	shut
			sing	sang	sung
make	made	made	sink	sank	sunk[9]
mean	meant	meant	sit	sat	sat
meet	met	met	sleep	slept	slept
mislay	mislaid	mislaid	slide	slid	slid
misspeak	misspoke	misspoken	slit	slit	slit
mistake	mistook	mistaken	speak	spoke	spoken
			speed	sped	sped

---

[4] The verb *hang* is irregular except when it means to execute by hanging. That verb is regular: He was hanged by the neck until dead.

[5] This verb can also be regular.

[6] *Proven* is the adjective form of *prove*: It's **a proven fact.**

[7] The intransitive verb *shine* is irregular; the transitive verb *shine*, however, is regular: He **shined** his shoes. His polished shoes **shone** beautifully.

[8] *Shrunken* is the adjective form of *shrink*: a shrunken head.

[9] *Sunken* is the adjective form of *sink*: They are looking for **sunken** treasure.

spend	spent	spent				
spill[10]	spilt	spilt		take	took	taken
spin	spun	spun		teach	taught	taught
spit	spat[11]	spat		tear	tore	torn
split	split	split		tell	told	told
spread	spread	spread		think	thought	thought
spring	sprang[12]	sprung		throw	threw	thrown
stand	stood	stood				
steal	stole	stolen		understand	understood	understood
stick	stuck	stuck		undertake	undertook	undertaken
sting	stung	stung		upset	upset	upset
stink	stank	stunk				
strike	struck	struck[13]		wake	woke	woken
string	strung	strung		wear	wore	worn
strive	strove	striven		weave	wove	woven
swear	swore	sworn		weep	wept	wept
sweep	swept	swept		win	won	won
swim	swam	swum		withdraw	withdrew	withdrawn
swing	swung	swung		write	wrote	written

---

[10] This verb can also be regular.
[11] Also: *spit/spit/spit*.
[12] Also: *sprung*.
[13] Form 3 can also be *stricken*, especially with illnesses: She was **stricken** with pneumonia.

SPELLING OF VERB FORMS

 Appendix B

Forms 2 and 3 of Regular Verbs

Type	Examples	Rule
Most regular verbs	visit + ed = visited predict + ed = predicted	Add -ed to most regular verbs.
Verbs ending in -y	worry + ed = worried marry + ed = married	Change the -y to i and add -ed.
Exception	play + ed = played enjoy + ed = enjoyed	If there is a vowel before the -y, do not change the -y to i.
Verbs ending in -e	received + ed = received love + ed = loved	Add only -d.

Activity 1   *Practice It!*

Write Form 2/3 of the following verbs.

Example:

love ⟶ loved

1. start	3. walk	5. advance	7. cry	9. destroy
2. marry	4. try	6. introduce	8. play	10. worry

Type	Examples	Rule
Verbs ending in one vowel and one consonant	pat + ed = patted permit + ed = permitted	Double the final consonant and add -ed.
Exception 1	fix + ed = fixed play + ed = played	Do not double x, w, or y.
Exception 2	picnic + ed = picnicked panic + ed = panicked	Add -ked to words ending in a hard c (a /k/ sound).
Exception 3	travel + ed = traveled open + ed = opened	If the word has more than one syllable and the stress is not on the final syllable, do not double the final consonant.

Activity 2　　*Practice It!*

Write Form 2/3 of the following verbs.

Example:

panic ⟶ panicked

1. stop
2. rob
3. permit
4. happen
5. occur
6. listen
7. offer
8. open
9. travel
10. omit

Form 4 of All Verbs

The following rules apply to all verbs except *be* and *have*.

Type	Examples	Rule
Most verbs	predict + s = predicts	Add -*s*.
Verbs ending in -*ch*, *sh*, -*ss*, -*z*, or -*x*	wish + s = wishes fix + s = fixes	Add -*es*.
Verbs ending in -*o*	do + s = does go + s = goes	Usually add -*es*, but check your dictionary to be sure.
Verbs ending in -*y*	marry + s = marries	Change the -*y* to *i* and add -*es*.
Exception	play + s = plays enjoy + s = enjoys buy + s = buys	If there is a vowel before the -*y*, add only -*s*. Make no other changes.
have	have + s = has	

Activity 3 *Practice It!*

Write Form 4 of these verbs.

Example:

play ⟶ *plays*

1. predict
2. go
3. wish
4. love
5. fall
6. mix
7. watch
8. employ
9. try
10. study

Form 5 of All Verbs

Type	Examples	Rule
Most verbs	work + ing = working	Add -*ing*.
Verbs ending in -*e*	smile + ing = smiling	Drop the -*e* and add -*ing*.
Exception	see + ing = seeing	If there is a double *ee*, do not drop the final -*e*.
Verbs ending in -*ie*	lie + ing = lying	Drop the -*ie* and add -*ying*.
Verbs ending in one vowel and one consonant	begin + ing = beginning shop + ing = shopping	In most cases, double the final consonant and add -*ing*.
Exception 1	fix + ing = fixing	Do not double *x*, *w*, or *y*.
Exception 2	picnic + ing = picnicking panic + ing = panicking	Add -*ked* to words ending in a hard *c* (a /k/ sound).
Exception 3	travel + ing = traveling happen + ing = happening	If the word has more than one syllable and the stress is not on the final syllable, do not double the final consonant.

Activity 4   *Practice It!*

Write Form 5 of these verbs.

Example:

play ⟶ *playing*

1. open
2. smile
3. fix
4. hit
5. begin
6. travel
7. lose
8. wish
9. sew
10. die

Activity 5   *Test It!*

Complete the following table.

Form 1	Form 2	Form 3	Form 4	Form 5
visit	*visited*	*visited*	*visits*	*visiting*
agree	___	___	___	___
call	___	___	___	calling
___	___	___	___	enjoying
___	___	kissed	___	___
___	___	___	lies	___
omit	___	___	___	___
___	___	___	opens	___
___	___	___	___	playing
prefer	___	___	___	___
___	___	reached	___	___
___	___	___	studies	___
___	___	___	travels	___
___	tried	___	___	___
wish	___	___	___	___

140

SUMMARY OF VERB TENSES

 Appendix C

The All-Time Tense: The Non-Focus

	Active Examples	Passive Examples
	People often **withdraw** money from their banks.	Money **is** often **withdrawn** from banks.

The Present Focus

	Active Examples	Passive Examples
Progressive present	Lonnie **is driving** her car.	The car **is being driven**.
Before-present	Ronny **has chosen** a video.	A video **has been chosen**.
Progressive before-present	Ronny **has been watching** TV for a while.	
After-present	Pearl **is going to withdraw** some money later today.	Some money **is going to be withdrawn** from Pearl's account later today.
Progressive after-present	People **are going to be eating** breakfast at 7:30 A.M. tomorrow.	

(Some passive tenses are omitted because they are never, or almost never, used.)

Past Focus

Simple past	Pearl **received** a great deal of money.	A great deal of money **was received** by Pearl.
Progressive past	People **were eating** breakfast at 7:30 A.M. yesterday.	Breakfast **was being eaten** at 7:30 A.M. yesterday.
Before-past	By 10:00 P.M. yesterday, Ronny **had watched** six videos.	Six videos **had been watched** by 10:00 P.M. yesterday.
Progressive before-past	When Burl returned to town, the police **had been investigating** him for months.	
After-past	Burl said that he **was going to withdraw** some money.	He said that some money **was going to be withdrawn.**
	Burl said yesterday that he **would clean** his gun.	He said that his gun **would be cleaned.**
Progressive after-past	Burl said yesterday that he **was going to be cleaning** his gun today.	
	Burl said yesterday that he **would be cleaning** his gug today.	

Simple future	Pearl **will withdraw** some money tomorrow.	Some money **will be withdrawn** tomorrow.
Progressive future with *will*	Pearl **will be withdrawing** money at 1:35 P.M. tomorrow.	
Before-future	By 11:30 tonight, Lonnie **will have driven** her car many miles.	By 11:30 tonight, Lonnie's car **will have been driven** many miles.
Progressive before-future	By 3:00 A.M. tomorrow, Lonnie **will have been driving** her car for many hours.	

INDEX